Testing an IT Service for Operational Use

IT Infrastructure Library

Ivor J Macfarlane
Richard Warden

Gildengate House,
Upper Green Lane,
NORWICH, NR3 1DW

London: HMSO

004.24 RT

© Crown Copyright 1993

Applications for reproduction
should be made to HMSO

First published   1993
ISBN   0 11 330560 5
ISSN   0956-2591

This is one of the books in the IT Infrastructure Library series. At regular intervals, further books will be published and the Library will be completed in 1993. Since many customers would like to receive the IT Infrastructure Library books automatically on publication, a standing order service has been set up. For further details on standing orders please contact:

HMSO Publicity (PU23 E3), FREEPOST,
Norwich, NR3 1BR
(*No stamp needed for UK customers*).

Until the whole Library is published, and subject to availability, draft copies of unpublished books may be obtained from CCTA if you are a standing order customer. To obtain drafts please contact:

IT Infrastructure Management Services
CCTA
Gildengate House, Upper Green Lane,
NORWICH, NR3 1DW.

For further information on other CCTA products, contact:

Press and Publications,
Room 3/9
CCTA
Gildengate House,
Upper Green Lane,
NORWICH, NR3 1DW.

This document has been produced using procedures conforming to
BS 5750 Part 1: 1987; ISO 9001: 1987.

Table of contents

1.	**Management summary**	**1**
1.1	Background	1
1.2	Testing an IT service for operational use	2
1.3	Benefits	2
2.	**Introduction**	**3**
2.1	Purpose	3
2.2	Target readership	4
2.3	Scope	4
2.3.1	Summary	4
2.3.2	A model of software testing	6
2.4	Related guidance	8
2.5	Standards	9
3.	**Planning for operational test management**	**11**
3.0	Concepts	11
3.1	Procedures	13
3.1.1	Appointing a Test Manager	14
3.1.2	Developing an implementation plan for operational testing	16
3.1.3	Performing risk and cost/benefit analyses	18
3.1.4	Aims and objectives	24
3.1.5	The awareness campaign	25
3.1.6	Developing procedures for operational testing	26
3.1.7	Developing procedures for system testing	36
3.1.8	Developing procedures for installation testing	41
3.1.9	Developing procedures for acceptance testing	43
3.1.10	Planning a pilot project	47
3.1.11	Expansion of the operational testing function	49
3.1.12	Management information and measurement	50
3.2	Dependencies	51
3.3	People	52
3.3.1	Organization	52
3.3.2	Operational Test Manager	54
3.3.3	Testing roles	54
3.3.4	Testing skills	55
3.3.5	Involvement of users	57
3.3.6	Involvement of other IT service management staff	57

3.3.7	Staffing levels required	58
3.3.8	Training and awareness	58
3.4	Timing	59

4. Implementing operational testing 61

4.1	Procedures	61
4.1.1	Pilot testing project	61
4.1.2	Ongoing implementation	63
4.2	Dependencies	65
4.3	People	66
4.4	Timing	66

5. Post-implementation and audit 69

5.1	Procedures	69
5.1.1	Reviewing objectives	70
5.1.2	Reviewing issues and problems	71
5.1.3	Audits	72
5.2	Dependencies	73
5.3	People	73
5.4	Timing	73

6. Benefits, costs and possible problems 75

6.1	Benefits	75
6.2	Costs	76
6.3	Possible problems	77

7. Tools 79

7.1	Introduction	79
7.2	Administrative tools	79
7.3	Test run support tools	80
7.4	Specialist tools	81

8. Bibliography 83

Table of contents

Annexes

A.	**Glossary of terms**	**A1**
B.	**Software lifecycles and operational testing**	**B1**
B.1	Introduction	B1
B.2	The V-model of testing activities	B1
B.3	Participation of operational testing in the SDLC	B3
C.	**Quality, testability and dependability**	**C1**
C.1	Introduction	C1
C.2	Quality	C1
C.2.1	Quality definitions	C1
C.2.2	Quality aims	C1
C.2.3	Basic quality rules	C2
C.3	Testability	C3
C.3.1	Maintainability	C4
C.4	Dependability	C4
C.4.1	When to stop testing	C5
C.4.2	The risk of change	C8
D.	**Checklists of basic handover requirements**	**D1**
D.1	Introduction	D1
D.2	Handover to operational testing	D1
D.3	Handover to software control and distribution	D2
D.4	General handover issues	D2
E.	**The principles of good testing**	**E1**
E.1	Preparing test plans	E1
E.2	Designing test suites	E2
E.2.1	Test suite design	E2
E.2.2	Test case design	E4
E.3	Preparing and executing test runs	E7
E.4	Analyzing test results	E8
E.5	Managing the test environment	E9
E.5.1	Using configuration management services	E10
E.5.2	Test environment design	E10
E.5.3	Test environment operation	E11
E.5.4	Test environment maintenance	E13

IT Infrastructure Library
Testing an IT Service for Operational Use

F.	**Formal signing off procedures**	**F1**
F.1	System tests	F1
F.2	Installation tests	F1
F.3	Acceptance tests	F2
G.	**Usability testing**	**G1**
G.1	Description	G1
G.2	Definitions and scope	G1
G.3	Applicability	G2
G.4	Methods used in usability testing	G3
G.5	Interface with problem management	G3
G.6	Summary	G4

Foreword

Welcome to the IT Infrastructure Library module on **Testing an IT Service for Operational Use.**

In their respective areas the IT Infrastructure Library publications complement and provide more detail than the IS Guides.

The ethos behind the development of the IT Infrastructure Library is the recognition that organizations are becoming increasingly dependent on IT in order to satisfy their corporate aims and meet their business needs. This growing dependency leads to growing requirement for quality IT services. In this context quality means 'matched to business needs and user requirements as these evolve'.

This module is one of a series of codes of practice intended to facilitate the quality management of IT services and of the IT Infrastructure. (By IT Infrastructure, we mean organizations' computers and networks - hardware, software and computer related communications, upon which application systems and IT services are built and run). The codes of practice will assist organizations to provide quality IT services in the face of skill shortages, system complexity, rapid change, growing user expectations, current and future user requirements.

Underpinning the IT Infrastructure is the Environmental Infrastructure upon which it is built. Environmental topics are covered in separate sets of guides within the IT Infrastructure Library.

IT infrastructure management is a complex subject which for presentational and practical reasons has been broken down within the IT Infrastructure Library into a series of modules. A complete list of current and planned modules is available from the CCTA IT Infrastructure Management Services at the address given at the back of this module.

The structure of the module is, in essence:

* a **Management summary** aimed at senior managers (Directors of IT and above, typically down to Civil Service Grade 5), senior IT staff and, in some cases, users or office managers (typically Civil Service Grades 5 to 7)

* the main body of the text, aimed at IT middle management (typically grades 7 to HEO)

* technical detail in Annexes.

The module gives the main **guidance** in sections 3 to 5; explains the **benefits, costs and possible problems** in section 6, which may be of interest to senior staff; and provides information on **tools** (requirements and examples of real-life availability) in section 7.

CCTA is working with the IT industry to foster the development of software tools to underpin the guidance contained within the codes of practice (ie to make adherence to the module more practicable), and ultimately to automate functions.

If you have any comments on this or other modules, do please let us know. A **Comments sheet** is provided with every module. Alternatively you may wish to contact us directly using the reference point given in **Further information**.

Thank you. We hope you find this module useful.

Acknowledgement

The assistance of the following contributors, all under contract to CCTA, is gratefully acknowledged:

Richard Warden and Paul Treble from the Centre for Software Maintenance Ltd

Dorothy Graham of Grove Consultants

Paul Herzlich of Système Evolutif

Ron Forster of PA Consulting

Robert Gale of Andersen Consulting.

We also wish to thank Martin Andrew and Maarten Kerssemakers, reviewing on behalf of the IT Infrastructure Management Forum.

Section 1
Management summary

1. Management summary

1.1 Background

Most organizations today rely totally upon their information systems to function; if those information systems do not support the business needs then the organization's business will suffer. IT services which fail to perform as expected are therefore a major concern, it is the role of the operational testing function to ensure, as cost effectively as possible, that a new or revised IT service will support the business needs for which it has been developed and thus reduce the risk to an organization's viability. This makes the operational testing function a vital factor in an organization's ability to survive.

Testing is an activity which should run throughout the development lifecycle of any new or revised software product. The historical image of testing as afterthought, an isolated function looking only at completed software, is giving way to a view of testing as an integral and pervasive aspect of the product lifecycle, working within structured development practices to improve the quality of IT services.

By designing acceptance tests at the same time as specifying requirements, those requirements can be tested conceptually against the needs of the business function being supported. This approach can (and in many progressive organizations does) save business analysts and software developers from building products which will not perform as required, helping to refine the stated requirements to more accurately reflect the business needs.

As IT becomes more embedded into the day-to-day business of an organization, so it becomes ever more essential to test the IT service as a whole; users see only the functionality and availability of the IT service, and see it only in terms of its success in satisfying their business needs. Concentrating too closely on the software within an IT service can lead to fault free software, but an unsatisfactory IT service. It is therefore essential that the service is tested as a whole, ensuring that all the components work together in a usable and consistent fashion. New concepts such as usability testing help address these concerns.

This book describes the process of planning for and implementing an operational testing function; directed at the operational testing of IT, whether supplied by in-house or external suppliers. In practice, most organizations following the guidance herein will find they are embarking upon a change of culture rather than the creation of a new unit; a redeployment and redesignation of staff, not a requirement to recruit additional staff.

1.2 Testing an IT service for operational use

This module covers the three elements of testing required prior to accepting new and/or amended IT services for operational use:

* **system testing**; demonstrating that an IT service meets the agreed requirements, and does so under all operating conditions

* **installation testing**; showing that the IT service is correctly installed in its live environment and meets the requirements of computer operations staff

* **acceptance testing**; gaining acceptance from users that the installed IT service meets their requirements, not only in terms of functions, but also in terms of usability.

1.3 Benefits

Benefits available from an efficient operational testing function include:

* confidence that a new or revised IT service meets the needs of the organization in terms of

    - service levels to customers

    - computer operations requirements

    - dependability

    - associated documentation

* improved software quality leading to more reliable services for the customers

* reduced costs of maintaining an IT service.

Not treating operational testing seriously can severely damage the business efficiency of the entire organization and lower staff morale, as well as wasting money by failing to learn from previous errors and repeating mistakes.

Section 2
Introduction

2. Introduction

This module has been written from the viewpoint of establishing a function to test IT services. In practice it is recognized that organizations will currently be carrying out testing of their IT services and will wish to amend and adapt that testing work in line with the guidance contained in this book.

It is not envisaged that extra staff will be required in the majority of organizations, rather that a new set of roles be identified to undertake the task, with staff being redesignated in order to achieve a better operational testing service than previously. The changes required will be primarily ones of culture and attitude, recognizing that testing is an activity which runs throughout a software lifecycle, not an isolated function taking place after software development has been completed.

2.1 Purpose

The aim of the operational testing function is to show that an IT service is suitable for operational use. To successfully complete the test, an IT service must:

* meet customer defined functional requirements

* meet customer defined non-functional requirements, such as service levels

* not have an adverse affect on other IT services.

The purpose of this module is to provide advice and guidance to senior IT managers and their staff on the planning and implementation of an efficient and effective operational testing function which will provide customers and IT service management staff with confidence in the quality and reliability of IT services. This embraces the following issues:

* identification of all the management elements which need to be considered at the planning and implementation stages of the operational testing function, such as costs, resources, staffing, organization and management reporting

* justification and establishment of the operational testing function

* integrating the test function with other software lifecycle activities such as analysis and maintenance, and identifying the necessary activities, methods and procedures to use for testing

* implementing the testing function in a controlled and manageable way.

2.2 Target readership

This module is specifically targeted at IT Services Managers and Operational Test Managers who are either establishing an operational testing function or wishing to review its practices. Additionally the module will be of interest and relevance to:

* IT Services Managers with responsibilities for
  - service level management
  - computer operations
  - network management
  - capacity management
  - availability management
  - configuration management
  - change management
  - software control and distribution

* IT Managers with responsibilities for
  - applications development
  - software maintenance

* customers with responsibilities for acceptance testing

* quality managers and audit staff.

2.3 Scope

2.3.1 Summary

The scope of this module is all aspects of the planning and implementation of a function for the operational testing of an IT service. All aspects of the IT service will require to be tested, not merely the software, nor indeed the IT elements. In order for an IT service to provide the functions, performance and availability required by the supported business function, the requirements specified must be

Section 2
Introduction

delivered in the operational environment. This means that the full extent of the Information System should be checked, this may include:

* IT equipment
* software
* documentation, covering
    - operating procedures
    - user manuals, templates and notes
    - help desk scripts
    - maintenance guidance
* human interfaces, including
    - user staff
    - management, both business and IT
    - IT staff
* information transfer facilities including
    - IT and telephone networks and associated equipment
    - postal facilities such as Post Office, courier services and internal messenger services
    - transfer of forms, paperwork and/or magnetic media between individuals/sections.

It should be clear from the above examples that an IT service may be produced with software that provides all the functionality and performance requirements specified but still does not 'do the job' in terms of supporting the business need. Consideration of the non-IT elements of the service in test design at an early stage of the lifecycle will help to ensure that the IT service is designed in such a way as to finally satisfy the business need. It will still be necessary, however, to carry out tests to ensure this is the case.

Operational testing is the verification and validation of systems, where validation is the process of determining whether software meets the customers' requirements, and where verification determines whether a system is being built correctly, eg meets the specification. Such testing, to be effective, must be carried out independently of the developer or maintainer producing the software. The independent test function should build upon tests carried out by the supplier of the software, increasing coverage and depth of testing, rather than duplicating previously documented testing.

In certain well-defined circumstances, eg Open Systems Environment products, the existence of accepted standard tests mean that testing by the supplier (first party testing) can be acceptable to a customer provided that the standard tests have been approved by the customer and the testing process is properly documented and made available to the customer.

Operational testing is a form of 'black box' testing, where testing staff require no knowledge of the internal structure or logic of the software. This is different to unit testing, which is often performed using 'white box' techniques, eg where specific logic paths are identified by examining the software, and then tests are designed and run to show whether or not these paths executed correctly.

2.3.2 A model of software testing

Figure 1, opposite, shows the major stages of testing an IT service. The stages may vary according to the software lifecycle model being implemented. The use of structured methods, such as SSADM, during development imposes an overhead, but the emphasis on structure and modularity it provides can make a significant contribution to all types of testing. Since requirements are structured in an hierarchy, the approach permits acceptance testing to relate directly to the business requirements as described in the requirements catalogue. The IT Infrastructure Library module **Software Lifecycle Support** gives more information about the use of lifecycle models.

Operational testing covers system, installation and acceptance testing, but it does not cover the development testing activities of unit and link test. In practice, the division between development and operational testing is often less clear-cut than might be implied by figure 1, with the early stages of system testing being carried out as the final part of developmental testing.

The figure shows the logical progression of testing, from module test to final acceptance. This is not meant to be interpreted as a strict sequential order. The figure does not show that some stages may be run concurrently, and that

Section 2
Introduction

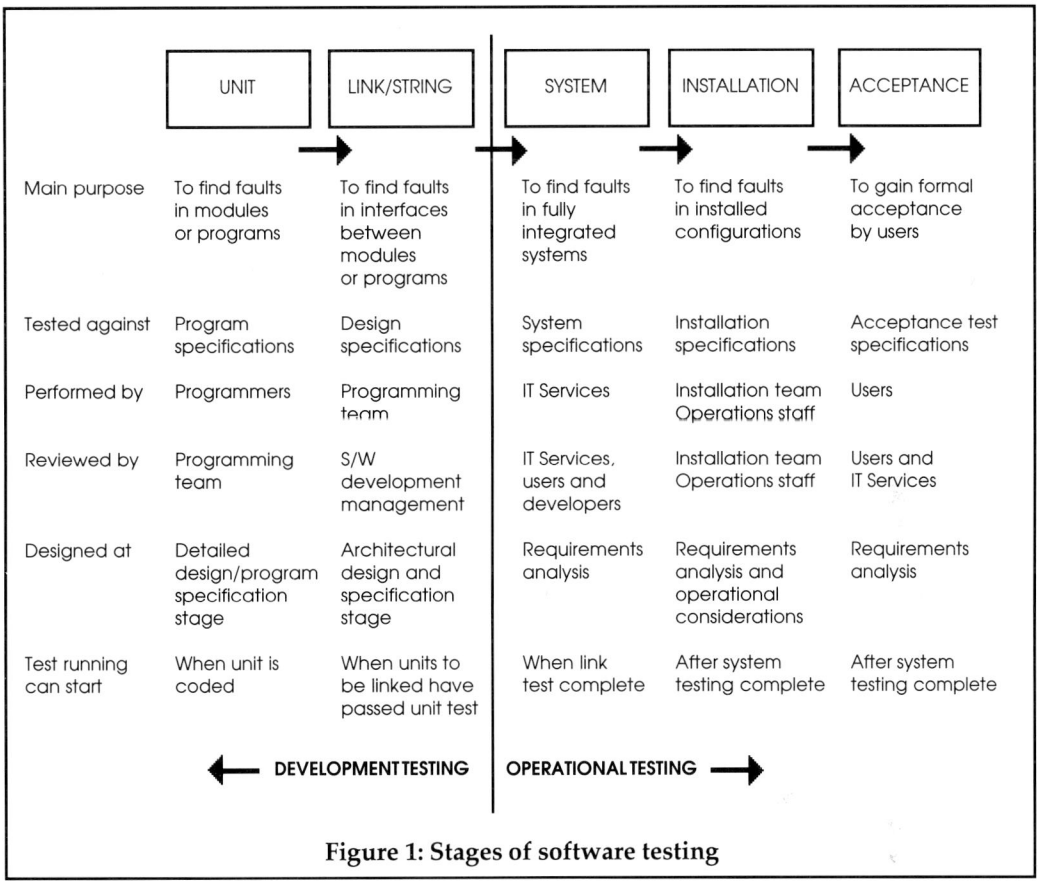

Figure 1: Stages of software testing

there may be iterations of one or more stages. The order and contents of each test stage may be modified by the requirement to start test execution as soon as possible.

It should also be realized that this simple picture will be heavily modified by the adoption of practices such as prototyping which remove much of the linearity from the lifecycle and demand a more iterative approach to testing, redesign etc.

Operational testing starts at the beginning of a project, with test specification and design activities, where projects range in size from a large multi-stage development for a new IT service to a minor maintenance change or enhancement to an existing IT service. The stages of testing, however, are still relevant.

The IT Infrastructure Library
Testing an IT Service for Operational Use

There are considerable benefits, in terms of cost and efficiency, from the consideration and design of tests at the requirements phase of the software lifecycle. Design of the tests which an IT service will be required to satisfy may aid the acceptance or rejection of a particular approach, clarify the requirements and identify areas where extra resource will be necessary.

After the earlier stages of test design have been completed, and once software has passed development tests, operational test running can commence. Many IT service management staff will be involved in some way with operational testing throughout the lifetime of an IT service. The module explains how to set up and maintain an appropriate infrastructure for managing test activities and link this to other IT service management functions.

Less emphasis is given to technical test methods, partly because they will vary significantly from one environment to another, but also because specific techniques cannot be put in place until the organization of the testing function has been determined. However, the annexes contain introductory descriptions to many well known methods, and the bibliography lists publications providing more detail.

2.4 Related guidance

This book is one of a series that constitute the CCTA **IT Infrastructure Library**. Although the module can be read in isolation, it is recommended that it is used in conjunction with other modules.

The following modules are considered to be particularly relevant.

Software Lifecycle Support describes how infrastructure management functions should be integrated in order to give support throughout the life of an IT service. More specifically, operational testers need to be involved from very early on in the software lifecycle.

The guidance contained in the **Service Level Management** module is relevant since one of the key aims of operational testing is to demonstrate that service levels can be achieved.

There is likely to be a need for IT capacity to run extensive tests, and also a need to test the capacity required by new or modified software. The **Capacity Management** module contains information relevant to both.

Section 2
Introduction

The guidance in the **Computer Operations Management** module is relevant since operations staff are involved in specifying software operability requirements, and subsequently in ensuring that the software meets those requirements.

Test designs and test files should be controlled using the guidance contained in the **Configuration Management** module. Ideally a single configuration management system is used to control the IT infrastructure, software and test data and scripts, the software being subject to the constraints and controls on release as described in the module addressing **Software Control and Distribution**.

Testing can create many changes, which need to be logged, tracked and reviewed, guidance on this is contained in the Library modules **Change Management** and **Problem Management**.

2.5 Standards

The following standards are relevant to testing activities:

BS5887 - Testing of Computer-based Systems

BS5515 - Documentation of Computer-based Systems

ISO8402 - Quality Vocabulary

ISO9126 - Information technology - Software product evaluation - quality characteristics and guidelines for their use.

ISO9001/EN29001/BS5750 Part 1 - Quality Management and Quality Assurance Standards

ISO9000 Part 3 - Guidelines for the application of ISO9001 to the development, supply and maintenance of software.

The IT Infrastructure Library modules are designed to assist adherents to obtain third-party quality certification to ISO9001. Organizations' IT Directorates may wish to be so certified and CCTA will in future recommend that Facilities Management providers are also certified, by a third-party certification body, to ISO9001. Such third-parties should be accredited by the NACCB, the National Accreditation Council for Certification Bodies.

In addition to the above extant standards, the BCS, via its Specialist Interest Group on software testing, is developing a standard on component testing.

The IT Infrastructure Library
Testing an IT Service for Operational Use

Section 3
Planning for operational test management

3. Planning for operational test management

This section gives guidance on the planning required prior to implementing an operational testing function as part of IT infrastructure management. The objective of the plan is to achieve a successful implementation by using appropriate hardware, personnel and tools at the right time.

3.0 Concepts

There are several concepts which require some explanation so that operational testing can be understood in context. They are dealt with here as a series of questions and answers.

Can testing prove that software is error free?

The short answer is NO, except for the most trivial cases. Any form of testing, whether at the program, system or operational level, has to acknowledge the fact that it is practically impossible to prove that software is error free. Whilst academic research has produced ways of showing small programs to be mathematically correct against a formal language specification, this approach is not viable for most commercial and scientific software. Consequently, operational testing should be designed in a way which gives the best test coverage and maximum confidence within the constraints of available resources and time.

What is the purpose of testing?

Testing has two aims which are complementary. The first is to identify and eradicate errors in software, and the second is to demonstrate that software is sufficiently error free that it can move to the next stage of the development or maintenance lifecycle. These aims focus testing efforts not simply on designing and running tests to show that software conforms to its specification, but on the more difficult task of demonstrating that the software conforms under as wide a set of conditions as can reasonably be tested.

What is the difference between testing and test running?

Testing describes the overall activity of test planning, analysis, specification, design, execution and review. Testing starts with the earliest lifecycle stages and continues throughout the lifecycle, with maintenance of test material continuing in parallel with maintenance of the software itself. Many potential errors in an IT service can be avoided by visualizing how a proposed IT solution to requirements would fare against the tests conceived. Additionally consideration of the tests an IT service must satisfy will help to refine the requirements, by linking them directly to the functionality and performance required by the finished product. Test running is the subset of testing which deals only with the execution and review of tests, which happens after the software has been built.

Annex B contains a more detailed description of testing, and shows how testing activities can be mapped onto a software lifecycle using the V-Model concept.

Does test running improve quality?

Test running alone cannot improve IT service quality. Its purpose is only to demonstrate the quality of the software under test. In this respect, test running is part of a larger process of error identification, correction and re-test.

However, testing in its widest sense does improve quality as it embodies activities such as reviewing software requirements and specifications in order to specify and design appropriate tests. These reviews can find errors, eg if there are ambiguities in a specification, then they will prevent test analysts from defining tests until the ambiguities are resolved. In general, testing improves quality by helping to ensure that software is designed to be both testable and maintainable.

What is the difference between verification and validation?

The ISO9000-3 definition for verification is "The process of evaluating software to ensure compliance with specified requirements". This can be interpreted as answering the question "Did we do what we said we'd do?"

Validation is defined by ISO9000-3 as "The process of evaluating the products of a given phase to ensure correctness and consistency with respect to the products and standards provided as input to that phase". This is related to the question "Did we build what we should have?"

What is the purpose of Operational Testing?

The purpose of operational testing is to demonstrate that an IT service will operate successfully within the actual business environment. From this it can be seen that operational testing encompasses both verification and validation.

Section 3
Planning for operational test management

What is a successful test?

There is more than one definition of a successful test. If there is an error in the IT service, then a successful test will find that error.

An unsuccessful test is one which fails to find an error when one exists in the IT service; where the error is subsequently found during operational running, the cost of correction will be considerably higher than had it been found by the testing process.

3.1 Procedures

The following procedures describe how to plan for an operational testing function. The main procedures cover the topics of:

* appointing an Operational Test Manager
* developing an implementation plan for the operational testing function
* performing a risk and cost/benefit analysis and determining dependability requirements for software
* agreeing aims and objectives
* conducting an awareness campaign
* developing procedures for testing
* planning a pilot project
* expansion of the function on an ongoing basis.

A vital consideration in designing procedures for successful testing is that test planning should start at the beginning of software development. Figure 2, overleaf, gives an example of the relationships between testing and the development stages.

Annex B discusses lifecycle models and the interactions with operational testing in more detail. In particular it discusses the V-Model of testing activities as a means of planning how testing work will integrate with the software development lifecycle. Additionally, the operational testing function will be involved with software development and maintenance via the project evaluation reviews of individual projects.

The IT Infrastructure Library
Testing an IT Service for Operational Use

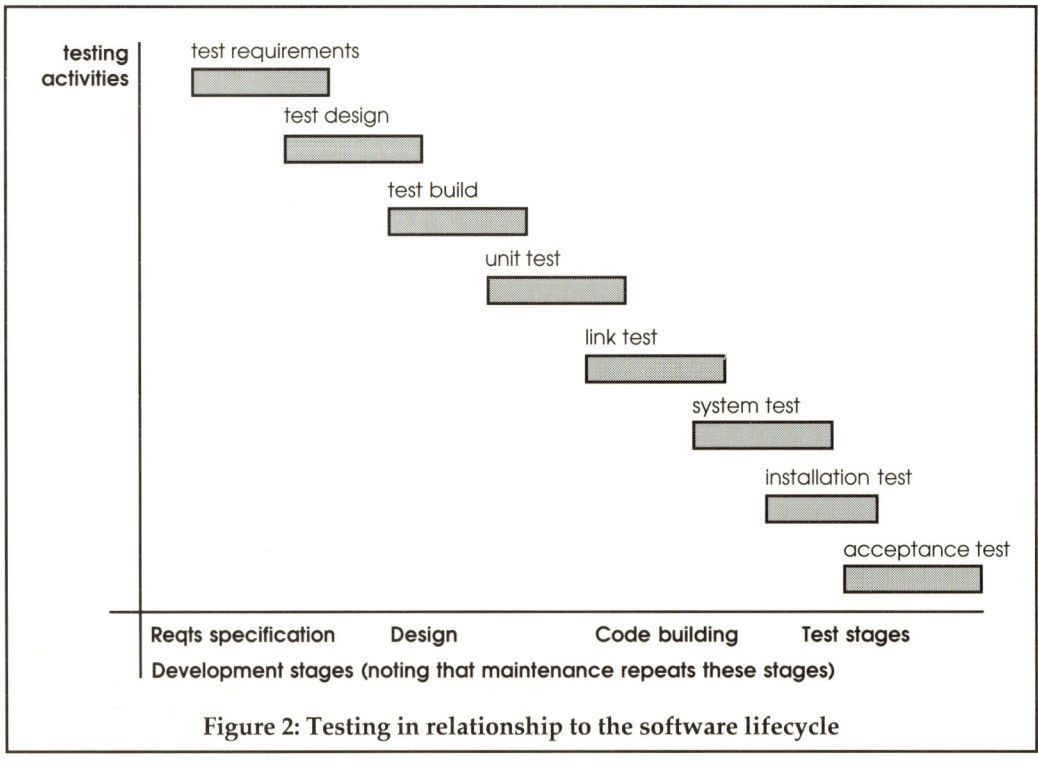

Figure 2: Testing in relationship to the software lifecycle

3.1.1 Appointing a Test Manager

The first step is to appoint an Operational Test Manager who will be responsible for planning and implementing a testing function which can perform:

* system testing
* installation testing
* acceptance testing.

The major responsibilities should include:

* developing and implementing a plan for the operational testing function
* establishing the cost/benefit case for the test function
* ensuring that all test plans and specifications are properly documented and maintained

Section 3
Planning for operational test management

* conducting a pilot project
* managing the whole testing function across all projects, including co-ordination with development and maintenance, scheduling and resourcing
* developing procedures for running operational tests on all new and updated IT services and related documentation, whether developed in-house or purchased by the organization
* staffing the test function and training of test personnel
* designing, implementing and maintaining test suites for IT services, as required by test plans
* producing regular management reports on test projects planned and in progress, eg establishing performance measures and producing information in the areas of software quality and performance measures, test team effectiveness and test team efficiency
* working with development and maintenance teams to ensure that operational test requirements are considered at the early stages of the software lifecycle
* liaising with customers and other IT service management functions, IT and departmental security officers to ensure that all are involved in the specification, execution and review of tests as appropriate
* ensuring that errors are reported and that appropriate re-testing is performed
* assessing new technologies and tools which may help to automate operational testing and increase productivity
* assessing new technologies being used in development and maintenance which may have an impact on test requirements and methods
* maintaining a knowledge of future demand for testing services.

For guidance on the qualities required in an Operational Test Manager please refer to section 3.3.2.

3.1.2 Developing an implementation plan for operational testing

The introduction (or reconstruction) of an operational testing function is a major area of work and it is recommended that a formal project is instigated to control the work. CCTA recommends the use of the PRINCE project management method for controlling such projects.

The following steps should appear in the implementation plan:

* assess current defect levels and costs in order to be able to estimate future benefits

* perform risk and cost/benefit analyses

* develop aims and objectives for the function and run an awareness campaign to publicize them, helping to ensure staff and users are aware of the importance of considering testing early in the lifecycle and the benefits to be gained from so doing

* appoint test managers who will be responsible for the three areas of test - system, installation and acceptance

* arrange for any training required to fill any gaps in the test manager's skills

* arrange for the installation of supporting computer systems

* develop and document testing procedures

* allocate and train staff needed to resource the pilot project

* identify, plan and implement a pilot project which will exercise all aspects of the function, noting that the test plan for the pilot will be a separate plan which is part of the software development plan for that project

* conduct a Post-Implementation Review of the pilot and assess the results against the original objectives, and decide whether full implementation of the testing function is to proceed

Section 3
Planning for operational test management

* finalize any changes to the operational testing function in the light of experience from the pilot project

* recruit and train additional staff needed for full implementation

* identify workloads and produce initial schedules in consultation with the development managers, making decisions about bringing projects already in progress into the new system

* establish a means to capture identified errors and improvements and a database to collect key system quality measures (this data will derive from individual testing projects but will provide measures which can be applied to the operational testing function and enable periodic reports to be produced for post-implementation monitoring - see section 5)

* ensure that test management systems and any tools or automated test facilities are operational

* determine the audit and review schedule required to monitor the full implementation of the operational testing function.

This list of steps is meant to be a guide, and will require interpretation and modification for use in a particular organization. For example, it is assumed above that separate test managers will be appointed for systems, installation and acceptance testing. In larger organizations this may be essential, whereas in smaller ones these roles may be combined.

3.1.2.1 Drafting an implementation plan

The Operational Test Manager should draft an initial implementation plan based upon the steps outlined above which covers the three stages of operational testing (as shown in figure 1, page 7). As each of these steps is performed, the plan can be revised.

The plan should cover not just the implementation schedule, but also the following key areas of information:

* overview of the operational testing needs of the organization

The IT Infrastructure Library
Testing an IT Service for Operational Use

* a proposed management structure for the operational testing function, identifying roles, responsibilities and relationships with software development, maintenance and other IT service management functions

* recommended procedures for system, installation and acceptance testing

* recommended number of staff, their skills requirements and costs

* recommended hardware configuration and costs

* recommended use of support tools and the degree of automated testing possible

* the expected benefits available from the restructuring of operational testing, which should be quantified wherever possible

* a summary of target costs, quality improvements and savings realizable from implementing the revised operational testing function.

3.1.2.2 Reviewing the plan with senior management

The plan should be reviewed regularly with senior management so that they can make informed decisions on how to continue with and develop the testing function. There will be important milestones when reviews should take place, and they should be documented in the plan. Examples are:

* on completion of risk and cost/benefit analyses

* on completion of a pilot test project

* periodically, as part of the plans for post-implementation review and audit.

3.1.3 Performing risk and cost/benefit analyses

The first step to be taken by the Operational Test Manager is the performance of risk and cost/benefit analyses for the operational testing function. Whilst senior IT management will have taken a decision to implement some form of operational testing function, a significant amount of work is required to assess the impact of errors in an IT service to the business, and to develop the details of the cost/benefit case for the function.

Section 3
Planning for operational test management

It is recommended that this study be carried out in four stages:

* a risk analysis, which examines the risks to the business associated with current testing methods, and identifies where an operational testing function can significantly reduce these risks

* an analysis of the benefits to the business of reducing these risks

* a gap analysis, which compares the current state of testing with the desired position, and identifies the direction that operational testing must take, and the associated resources and costs needed to implement the function

* a risk assessment, which compares the reduction of risk expected from the function against the costs of implementation.

The major benefit of these analyses is that they first specify the business needs for an operational testing function, and then match the requirements of the new testing function to those needs. This permits a goal oriented approach to the planning and introduction of operational testing, which is important as it ensures that any benefits can be related back to business objectives.

Use of a risk management method such as CRAMM can assist by quantifying the identified risks, facilitating comparison of risks.

The following sections give guidance on how to perform each of these analyses.

3.1.3.1 Risk analysis

Risk analysis is a useful technique for assessing the impact of poor quality IT services on various aspects of an organization's business. (This applies to impacts upon the business of both customer and supplier.) Working within an IT Directorate, it is easy to lose sight of the fact that the ultimate objective is to maintain and improve the support given to customers by the IT services. Risk analysis can be used to focus attention on topics which might be affected by the inability of an IT service to meet the stated requirements:

* loss of business if an organization is unable to trade

The IT Infrastructure Library
Testing an IT Service for Operational Use

* political or corporate embarrassment, ie where an organization might be seen as acting in an unprofessional manner, eg issuing incorrect invoices or payments, or the issuing of inaccurate data or information, requiring subsequent public retraction

* loss of commercial confidentiality, eg where software errors allow unauthorized access to new product designs

* infringement of personal privacy, eg where software errors allow unauthorized access to personnel data in contravention of the Data Protection Act

* personal safety hazards, eg where errors in medical records software leads to the false recording of radiation treatment, with the risk that patients may be given overdoses of ionising radiations

* failure to meet legal obligations, eg failure to make financial company returns or make statutory payments

* financial loss, eg where errors in accounting software permit fraud.

Risk analysis should focus initially on the numbers, frequency, effects and costs of software errors which have been encountered in live running. From this information the analysis should then consider where current testing methods are weak; that is, where a lack of proper testing increases the risk of live software errors.

Relevant information may be gathered from a number of infrastructure management functions which are usually involved when errors affect live IT services. They may include:

* service level management, which can provide data on current service levels, and where they fail to meet business needs

* availability management, which can provide data on software reliability

* Help Desk, whose records can be used to determine the number and types of problems which users have reported

* problem management, which can provide data on the costs and causes of service failures

Section 3
Planning for operational test management

> * computer operations management and network management, which can provide data on the effects of service failures and software errors on the ability to maintain operational services.

In addition the risk analysis will require an examination of current testing methods, both in development and maintenance work. This examination should look for any relationships between the quality of the software, and the frequency and types of errors found during operational running.

Annex C discusses quality, testability and dependability in more detail. Whilst risk reduction may be a prime motive for introducing an operational testing function, Annex C discusses the following specific requirements:

* risk factors should be reflected in software requirements and specifications for an IT service but operational testing should also look for risks which are not documented

* software must be designed to be testable, otherwise operational testing cannot provide an effective risk reduction service

* determining the point at which software dependability is acceptable and testing can stop is difficult, but essential, for cost effective testing.

The main output of the analysis should be a report which summarizes the current risks to the business which can be attributed to inadequate operational testing.

3.1.3.2 Benefits analysis

The next stage is to perform a benefits analysis for the proposed operational testing function. With the risk analysis as the major input it is necessary to determine how operational testing can reduce risks, and how this increased dependability will benefit the business.

Benefits analysis has to contain some degree of speculation and judgment as it employs hypothetical scenarios based upon historical data. The major question that has to be considered is, "if operational testing had been applied to past projects, what effect could it have had in reducing service failures, and what would have been the benefit to the business of this?"

The IT Infrastructure Library
Testing an IT Service for Operational Use

Relevant performance measures to support this might include:

* number of corrective changes applied to released IT services

* errors detected at installation and/or acceptance test that could have been detected at system testing

* lost availability of an IT service to users.

From risk analysis it should be possible to identify the types and frequency of past service failures which operational testing would seek to prevent in the future; and to assess the ability to eradicate failures from an IT service before release and at what cost this might be achievable. Using historical data an estimate should be made of the costs in terms of:

* business operations having to live with errors in an IT service

* the IT Directorate rectifying errors

* loss of customers and customer opportunities.

It is acknowledged that in some circumstances measuring these costs may be secondary. The imperative may simply be to introduce operational testing to prevent particularly severe types of service failure from recurring.

Two assertions need to be made in order to quantify the benefits:

* that operational testing will minimize these types of failure in the future

* that without an operational testing function the past trends of service failures will continue.

3.1.3.3 Gap analysis

A gap analysis is used to determine any deficiencies between the existing approach and practices in operational testing, and those recommended by this module.

As there is no specific technique which can be recommended for performing a gap analysis, the following steps are suggested:

* document the current test environments in terms of methods, techniques and tools, resources and costs

Section 3
Planning for operational test management

* identify any performance measures used which can give an insight into current test effectiveness and efficiency such as

    - service unavailability due to errors

    - number and cost of corrective maintenance projects

    - cost of testing compared to errors found at each stage

* consider the information collected in the risk analysis in order to determine acceptable dependability levels

* consider the benefits analysis to determine the implementation priority for the testing function.

The gap analysis should be used to prepare a report in which the deficiencies between existing practice and the procedures and practice recommended in this book are documented. It should detail the skills required and estimate the staff and computer resources needed to make necessary improvements. Also include budget figures for the cost of implementation, and indicate whether these costs would be justified in terms of realizable benefit to the organization. Where it is not possible to consider full implementation of operational testing, the report should also prioritize those areas where the greatest benefits are anticipated.

3.1.3.4 Risk assessment

The risk assessment consolidates the results of the previous three analyses in order to answer the question, "What are the cost/benefit cases which support the implementation of an operational testing function?"

Any cost/benefit case has to consider the law of diminishing returns, identifying when the costs of testing exceed the value of the benefits.

There may be a number of ways of presenting the cost/benefit case, depending on how the operational testing function is to be implemented. For example the highest risks, and costs, may be associated with a small proportion of the IT service. Therefore there will be a strong cost/benefit argument in favour of implementing the operational testing function on a selective basis. Alternatively, the cost/benefit analysis may support implementation for all IT services.

The IT Infrastructure Library
Testing an IT Service for Operational Use

The risk assessment should present senior IT management with the various options, so that a decision can be made on both whether, and where, operational testing is to be implemented. The objective is to obtain firm management commitment to the formation and running of the operational testing function, therefore any presentation must convey solid evidence of the benefits that the operational testing group will bring to the organization in achieving its overall business goals.

3.1.4 Aims and objectives

Once the decision to proceed with an operational testing function has been made, the Operational Test Manager should prepare aims and objectives. This will help to clarify the purpose of the operational testing function.

The culture within certain organizations may make it desirable to produce a mission statement for the operational testing function, to encapsulate its envisaged role. Where this is done, the resulting statement should be publicized as widely as possible throughout the organization. The Operational Test Manager or IT Services Manager should, in any case, produce documented aims for the operational testing function and agree these aims with customer and IT management.

More detailed objectives need to be documented, along with associated performance measures. The risk and cost/benefit analysis should provide the input for determining these objectives. A key purpose of objectives is that they provide the criteria to be used when performing Post-Implementation Reviews (see section 5).

Some examples of objectives are:

* reduced risks to the business through the increased dependability (measured in terms of the number of errors detected in those IT services which have most impact on business operations)

* improvements in the effectiveness of testing, as measured by the cost of testing versus the number of errors found

* improvements in service levels, as measured by the reduction of errors found in live running, and also by improved systems availability and reduced calls on Help Desk and problem management services

* improved software reliability, through earlier detection and removal of errors

Section 3
Planning for operational test management

* reduced costs of software development and maintenance from reducing expensive rework caused by the late detection of software errors, and using the results of testing as feedback to the development process.

3.1.5 The awareness campaign

The next stage in the planning procedure is for the Operational Test Manager to run an awareness campaign.

The main reason for running an awareness campaign is that an operational testing function will have an impact on both the work of most IT staff, and on the customers. Therefore it is essential that all staff understand why the function is being introduced, how it will affect them, and what the benefits to them and the organization will be.

It is recommended that the campaign be organized as a series of presentations given to staff over a period of not more than two months. Whilst all presentations should describe the reasons for the function and its objectives, they should be targeted at three audiences:

* customers, who should be given a business and operational perspective of operational testing

* IT management, who need to understand the effects of operational testing on their own management responsibilities

* IT staff, who need to understand how the function will affect their own work.

Whilst the Operational Test Manager will play the major role in organizing and presenting an awareness campaign, senior management support is required in at least three ways to:

* provide active support for the campaign so that operational testing is given a high profile within the organization

* ensure that all staff are given the opportunity to attend meetings

* play a visible role by being actively involved in the presentations to staff of the proposed operational testing function.

The IT Infrastructure Library
Testing an IT Service for Operational Use

There is further information in the IT Infrastructure Library module on **Customer Liaison** about running publicity and awareness campaigns.

3.1.6 Developing procedures for operational testing

This section discusses issues which are common to the system, installation and acceptance stages of operational testing, under the headings:

* common planning requirements
* interfaces to software development and maintenance
* interfaces to users
* test data
* IT service architecture
* software upgrades
* obtaining good test coverage
* test management systems.

The following issues need to be addressed individually for the system, acceptance and installation stages of operational testing, namely:

* objectives
* range of testing
* hardware and software resources required.

They are discussed for each type of testing in sections 3.1.7 to 3.1.9.

3.1.6.1 Common planning requirements

Each of the operational test types need to be planned so that they are integrated with the software lifecycle. Figure 2, on page 14, illustrates the main relationships between testing and the lifecycle and this relationship is used here as a basis for a test plan.

Before operational testing commences, the Operational Test Manager should be satisfied that all the appropriate stages of development testing have been carried out, ie:

* requirements stage including
    - initial development of the test plan

Section 3
Planning for operational test management

        identification of overall test requirements; most importantly the dependability levels required of the software, and degree of confidence needed that these levels have been met, established by customers' identification of the criticality of these services to the business functions

- review of test requirements against the software requirements

* specification stage, comprising

    - decomposition of test requirements into the test cases required to meet each software specification

    review of these tests against the specifications

* design stage, consisting of

    - design and building detailed tests

    - reviewing these tests against the software design

* coding stage, including

    - building test environments for operational testing

    - reviewing those test environments.

The operational testing stage of the test plan would comprise:

* perform system testing

* review test results

* perform installation testing

* review test results

* perform acceptance testing

* review test results

* system handover to the customer.

The final element of the plan will be to allow for a Post-Implementation Review, to establish any inadequacies identified or improvements required.

A number of points need to be made about this plan:

* the development of test requirements, test designs and test cases is required for each type of operational testing (ie system, installation and acceptance testing)

27

* within the software development lifecycle, operational tests may need to be performed several times before the software can be considered suitable for live running

* projects may be phased, which in turn requires that operational testing is phased to support the handover of different parts of the software to the customers at different times in the project plan

* system, installation and acceptance tests should be planned and designed to avoid duplication, maximize coverage and use common test cases where practicable

* acceptance testing of a replacement system may have to include parallel running with the original system

* during the maintenance stages operational testing will be repeated many times.

The outline planning steps described here can be developed by an organization into a generic test plan which can then be tailored to specific projects.

3.1.6.2 Interfaces to software development and maintenance

Defining the interface between the operational testing function and the software development teams (which includes maintenance teams if maintenance is organized separately) is of prime importance to the overall success of the operational testing function. It is important that the software developers view operational test design and test running as essential and complementary activities to their own work.

Procedures are required for test analysis, design, build, running and quality assurance of the test cases and test designs, to ensure that testing staff are involved at the appropriate time with software development and maintenance staff. The specific tasks of the testing staff, and the involvement of developers and maintainers should be clearly defined. These procedures may form part of a quality management system, as they describe quality control activities.

Operational test running starts when the software development team has successfully completed unit and link testing. These stages should have comprehensively tested all programs and modules and their interfaces.

Section 3
Planning for operational test management

There should be a formal handover of each deliverable, as listed in Annex D, from software development to operational testing unit to ensure that the status of software entering operational testing is recorded. The more controlled this process is, the less likely it will be that problems will arise. Use of version numbers, to identify the status of each software release, is an essential part of this control process. The system test teams should check that all the required products have been delivered. In particular they should confirm that appropriate unit and link tests have already been run, and that the results are available for analysis. Records of software errors that caused the most frequent and serious problems in these earlier tests can be used to help direct the system testing effort to the areas of greatest concern. The system tests should not simply be a mere duplication of the earlier tests, but carry a different emphasis, in addressing the function of the IT service as a whole, rather than testing the software in isolation.

At handover stage there should, ideally, be no known errors in the software, though in practice circumstances may dictate that agreement (between software development, operational testing and customers) is reached for software with known minor errors to be passed to operational test, on the understanding that these errors will be fixed in a later release.

Criteria for referral back to software development should be established. If a large number of problems, attributable to poor testing at earlier stages is encountered during testing, the operational test teams must pass software back for rework rather than continue to pour effort into testing software that is inevitably going to be subject to substantial change.

3.1.6.3 Interface to users

Since the purpose of an IT service is to support the business needs of its users, those users are best qualified to assess whether or not the IT service meets its requirements. In practice, senior users often perform the role of customer, being vested with the accept/reject decision on a new or revised IT service.

There will in many cases be (at least the potential for) legal and financial implications regarding the acceptance of an IT service. Therefore the scope and nature of tests, together with the procedure for performing test runs and resolving any errors must be agreed beforehand. Users will have been involved in the design of tests early in the lifecycle and this involvement should be maintained throughout the operational testing process. User involvement will increase during the running of acceptance tests, including:

* skilled users, who are in a position to establish whether the IT service fulfils the business needs described in the specification

* unskilled users who can assess the ease with which the new or revised practices (not just the IT components) can be picked up

* management's acceptance of the product on a value for money basis.

Criteria should be agreed, as a part of the requirements specification, between the software supplier and the user, covering:

* acceptance of the IT service (ie an acceptable error level)

* rejection criteria, at which test running will cease and the product be returned to the software developers

* repair situations, where test running may continue whilst the IT service is amended to correct identified errors.

Test plans should be designed to ensure that errors are identified as a result of running the tests rather than when the system is operational. Real problems should be investigated for reproducibility and recorded by the test team in such a way that they can be effectively resolved by the development or support team.

Once the IT service has met the acceptance criteria there should be a formal handover of the system by the supplier to the user during which acceptance documents are signed.

3.1.6.4 Test data

It is generally neither appropriate nor sufficient to use a copy of the live database to constitute test data since it is unlikely to provide the necessary broad coverage of the system under test. By its nature, live data will produce a high preponderance of normal transactions, whereas many errors arise from exception handling procedures. Copies of live databases can prove more useful in high volume and load testing, offering an attractive means of producing a large quantity of relevant data cheaply. It is necessary to

Section 3
Planning for operational test management

achieve a correct balance between the cost of developing special data and scripts compared with the disadvantages of using cheap available data.

Particular care must be taken to ensure that this data is accorded the same level of security protection as it would attract were it being processed as live data. Test prints may contain information of sensitive or confidential nature, even where figures etc on the live database have been altered.

3.1.6.5 IT service architecture

The complexity of IT service architecture may have a significant effect on the degree of operational testing required, for example where one or more of the following applies to an IT service:

* geographically separate sites
* distributed processing
* distributed databases.

Operational testing then becomes more difficult to plan, and more time-consuming to execute. For example, both system and acceptance tests may need to be run on each geographical site in order to demonstrate that the IT service runs correctly from any location on a network. Additionally, it will be vital that any cross-site links are tested, together with any transportability requirements, including requirements in support of contingency plans.

Procedures for installing software on multi-site systems are likely to be more complicated and time-consuming to set up than those on single-site systems.

3.1.6.6 Software upgrades

Whenever a software upgrade is produced, the integrated IT service must be examined and a suitable testing plan devised. In general software upgrades are more complex to deal with than new software since their effect on existing data, installation procedures and operational procedures must be taken into account. The organization's change management policy will control the frequency of upgrades.

Furthermore, change management information can be used to determine whether particular changes warrant a retest of the entire system (full hierarchy) or whether testing should be restricted to those areas which may be affected by the change (impacted hierarchy).

The IT Infrastructure Library
Testing an IT Service for Operational Use

Upgrades may take many forms, for example changes in:

* bespoke software developed in-house or externally
* off-the-shelf packaged applications
* system software
* communications software
* database management software
* hardware
* data sets imported from other systems.

Test plans should ensure that provision is made for all the necessary system, installation and acceptance tests to be designed and executed.

The software maintenance process recognizes four classes of software change that will result in upgrades. These are:

* **corrective maintenance**; correcting an error found during live running
* **perfective maintenance**; where there are additions, modifications or deletions to the functions of the software to correspond with changes in the business requirement
* **adaptive maintenance**; to allow for changes to the environment such as new systems software or new hardware, but where the functions of the IT service are not changed
* **preventive maintenance**; carried out to make the software easier to maintain (or to test) in the future.

All changes that result from maintenance must pass through their own development cycle of designing, coding and testing. The requirements for testing changes are, if anything, more stringent then those for new systems. Not only must errors be found in the operation of the features affected by the change but questions such as "Has anything been left out?" and "What other parts of the system are affected?" must also be answered.

The principles of good testing (see Annex E) should be applied to testing changes. In theory for each set of changes all operational system, installation and acceptance tests should be repeated with additions and/or modifications to test the correct functioning of the changes. In practice such full hierarchy testing will consume too much time and effort to be practical if the tests are not automated. The alternative is to assess the impact of any change in terms of its implications for functionality, performance, volume, documentation etc, and run tests aimed at finding errors in the impacted hierarchy.

Irrespective of whether or not full or impacted hierarchy techniques are used, many of the tests will be repeated each time a change is made. The test procedures should ensure that selected tests are run again as regression tests. The purpose of these tests is to provide assurance that those parts of the system that should be unchanged are indeed unchanged. Thus regression tests do not necessarily need to test all aspects of the IT service, but can be selected to check those judged to be most important. The need for regression tests to be run each time a change is made makes them an obvious candidate for automation.

3.1.6.7 Methods of obtaining good test coverage

Effective operational testing requires both depth and breadth of coverage. Depth is provided by the rigour of the test cases and test designs, and can be provided by skilled testers and other infrastructure management function staff applying the principles of good testing described in Annex E. Breadth is dependent on the nature of the IT service, the software involved, the architectural complexity etc, but can be assisted by having as many people as possible from different backgrounds involved in planning and executing operational testing. Consideration should be given to ways of achieving good breadth of coverage. The purpose of obtaining good test coverage is to ensure that the software has been adequately tested before handover; methods to help include:

* beta site testing in cases where the system will be used on many sites
* pilot running of the new or upgraded systems
* parallel running of the new and old systems.

Beta site testing

Beta site testing is mainly applicable to software products where:

* the software will be installed in a large customer base, usually spread over a large number of installations

* full acceptance testing is not possible on every site
* the supplier needs some form of external and independent test running of the software prior to its full release.

In this form of test running, software will have completed system and installation testing, and is released to a small number of carefully selected customers for a specified period of time. These customers will run the software as normal, and report any errors or problems to the supplier.

Beta site testing is often used as a final test for software products, where it is not feasible for every customer to be involved in acceptance testing.

Pilot running

Pilot running of a new or upgraded system is a form of controlled implementation. It differs from beta testing in that, while beta testing is run in several sites, usually selected by the supplier, pilot running involves one site, normally selected by the customer.

Even though the software has completed acceptance testing, if it is to be run by a large number of users, perhaps in several or many geographically separate sites, it may be considered too risky for all users to move to the new software in one go.

Consequently, a pilot project is run, installing and live running the IT service by a controlled number of users for some specified period of time, with the aim of additional confidence building. It is a form of extended acceptance testing confined to one early implementation at one site.

Parallel running

Parallel running of the new and old systems is used mainly when there has been a major redevelopment of the system, perhaps with a complete change of hardware and systems software.

With large systems it may be very difficult to demonstrate that the new system provides an equivalent operational service to the old system, as well as providing new functions and services. This objective can be achieved by a period of live parallel running. During this time the same inputs will be used by each system, and all outputs will be compared to ensure that the new system is functioning correctly. Users and operations staff will be comparing the new system with the old to ensure that their requirements are still being met by the new software.

If the new system is accepted, then it can replace the old system. If it is not, then the old system can continue to provide the live services.

Parallel running is a very expensive form of testing. However the cost is often justified by the large degree of user confidence it can inspire. Alternative approaches are possible, such as saving and using historical data during an extended acceptance trial. Effectively this constitutes 'retrospective parallel running'. Whilst this may not have the same initial demonstration of confidence to customers it should have the same degree of test coverage. Parallel running inevitably impacts upon the service provided to users and upon the service they in turn are able to provide to their customers. The benefits and confidence that can result from parallel running must therefore be carefully balanced against the impact to the business of extensive overheads in terms of cost and delays. An error free IT service will not be desirable at the cost of corporate bankruptcy.

3.1.6.8 Test management systems

While operational testing is in progress, control must be maintained over the versions of software, documentation, test data and test plans in use. This is an area where computerization of the operational testing records may be appropriate. If the organization has implemented configuration management then the controls may already be available. If not, then their provision should be considered.

Annex E (E.5) discusses test management systems in more detail, under the headings of:

- *   configuration management services
- *   design
- *   operation
- *   maintenance.

3.1.7 Developing procedures for system testing

Procedures for system testing (the range of which is described in 3.1.7.1) should be developed to satisfy the following objectives:

* test a fully developed IT service in which all parts are present, including software, documentation and associated hardware; that is the configuration of the IT service is as close to that of the final operational system as possible

* maximize the test coverage of system functions, in order to maintain a high level of confidence in the software

* minimize the costs of testing without reducing the amount of testing performed

* establish whether service levels are going to be met in the live IT service.

3.1.7.1 Range of testing

The range of testing required to fully test the IT service may be substantial, and it will have a significant impact on the planning, implementation and resourcing of the system testing function. The following headings provide a checklist.

Function

System testing tests the IT service as a whole in its ability to meet the specified requirements and hence support the business function or functions concerned. Unit and link testing will have tested components of the IT service and individual program interfaces, it is only when all of the components are configured as for the live IT service that complete transactions can be tested through all of their processing steps.

Load/stress

The software should be operated at varying load conditions, including peak loads, eg the maximum number of users, or simulated users, specified for a network log-on simultaneously, to ensure that the IT service meets the maximum load specification and transaction throughput.

Section 3
Planning for operational test management

Volume

An IT service should be run with high volumes of input data under continuous load conditions, eg fill a database file with the maximum amount of data specified and then subject it to a very high transaction rate.

Hardware configuration and portability

Where an IT service runs across a range of hardware configurations, additional tests may be required to show that the software functions correctly in each of these configurations. These tests should show that:

* the software can be ported onto the required hardware

* where different versions of software are required to support different hardware platforms, these versions are correctly controlled by the configuration management system

* the associated documentation covers all the hardware platforms concerned.

Database loading and data conversion

For system testing to proceed, it may be necessary to load databases with appropriate data and/or convert existing data to new formats that are applicable for use with the new system. Separate utilities are normally used to perform these functions, and tests should be devised to check data integrity.

Security

Tests should be devised to specifically check the required security features of the system; do the access, integrity and recovery features function as expected? The range of security testing may be extensive for large, multi-site networked systems. This can be a specialized activity and should be performed with support from the departmental and IT security officers. Furthermore, access to database files may need to conform to legal requirements laid down in the Data Protection Act.

Performance

Tests should be performed which assist staff to look for circumstances in which the IT service does not perform as required in the product specifications, eg check response times and throughput rates under peak and continuous loads. There is a need to define 'normal load' conditions in order to assess the acceptability of response times.

Availability

Testing is required to show that the IT service meets its reliability objectives. Any errors should be noted and the mean time between failures measured. The second step is to measure the mean time taken to repair. Availability, or the lack of it as expressed in downtime, can then be assessed from a combination of these measures. Details of the appropriate calculations and their interpretation is contained in the **Availability Management** module.

Race conditions

The IT service may have been designed on the basis that transaction or input types have to be processed in a particular sequence. However it may be possible to input these transactions out of sequence. For example in an interactive networked IT service, transactions on the same database record may be input simultaneously, and a race ensues where it is not possible to predict the order in which the inputs will be processed. Tests should be designed to show whether the software reacts correctly to inputs which are out of sequence.

Recovery

If recovery and contingency plans have been developed, tests should be performed to exercise these plans. Whereas availability testing examines the effects of individual errors on system availability, recovery is concerned with more catastrophic failures which are often due to external factors, rather than software related. For example, if the computer hardware fails completely, the contingency plan may be to reload the software and databases onto another machine on the same site, or even to use an alternative site. Where new or revised IT services are significant, the contingency plan for existing IT services will require appropriate amendment and testing. Reference should be made to the **Contingency Planning** module which gives further advice on testing contingency plans.

Hardware maintainability

There may be instances where the software can assist in the servicing and testing of hardware. For example the software may contain device drivers for special output devices such as plotters, and running these drivers can be included in hardware servicing procedures. Any special tests such as

Section 3
Planning for operational test management

this should be run and checked to ensure that they will support any servicing requirements. Such software is often proprietary and as such cannot be tested by its users except in so far as it supports the IT service as a whole.

Interfaces

Every IT service has procedural interfaces which describe how the service interfaces with other parts of the organization. Sometimes these interfaces are to other IT services, but inevitably the IT procedures are also required to interact with manual and/or clerical procedures. These procedures should, where appropriate, be subject to equal attention during operational testing, to ensure that the entire Information System (not just the IT aspects) continues to function with the new or changed IT service component.

Documentation

There may be substantial documentation with the software, including user manuals, update notes, operations procedures, on-line documentation and help facilities, and help desk guides. Part of the process of system testing is to ensure the accuracy, completeness and usability of all associated documentation.

Human factors

In the operational testing of an IT service, it must not be forgotten that part of that IT service comprises staff. It is important that the human aspects of the IT service are designed to work with the IT aspects and test design should follow accordingly. The interfaces of the IT service with affected staff, (IT staff such as help desk operators as well as users) should be tested before live running whenever and as fully as practicable.

The ease with which an IT service can be used is an important element in the value which that IT service can ultimately offer to the organization. Testing of usability should address the needs of the whole range of potential users, covering different levels of experience, skill levels, language differences etc. A brief description of the concepts of usability testing is included as Annex G. Usability requirements should have been included as part of the requirements specification.

The IT Infrastructure Library
Testing an IT Service for Operational Use

3.1.7.2 Hardware and software resources required

It is essential for the system test group to have access to hardware which allows them to carry out the full range of system tests listed above. Access to large amounts of disk, memory space or user terminals may be required for some volume or stress/load testing while other tests will require access to the complete range of peripherals that may be used. Some items of hardware may be shared with live services where no disruption is anticipated, alternatively there may be separate hardware for development and testing.

In some circumstances test staff may need hardware and software to be reconfigured. For example, they may need peripherals to be removed from the system in order to check how software functions if those peripheral are not available.

When new software is being tested there is a high likelihood that system crashes will occur. Indeed testers will be actively seeking to find conditions in which the IT service does crash. Therefore the test environment must be designed so that crashes do not affect either the test schedule or other activities on site, especially live IT services. These considerations point to the desirability of a separate computer or test environment, and/or the scheduling of tests outside business hours.

If the IT service is designed to run on a range of hardware configurations then as many of the configurations as possible must be made available to the system test team. In practice it may be impossible to test all possible configurations but usually an appropriate choice and mix will minimize the risk of operational problems later.

There may be times when for physical or cost reasons, all parts of an IT service will not be available for testing purposes at all times. In these circumstances the use of simulation tools (hardware or software) can be considered for some of the testing with a final (hopefully short) test with the real components in place. A typical example might be where a new network is being installed, but will not be available at system testing time.

Section 3
Planning for operational test management

3.1.8 Developing procedures for installation testing

In developing installation testing procedures, the following objectives must be addressed:

* to find errors in any installation procedures and their associated documentation where the procedures have been used for installing software and hardware into the live environment

* to minimize the costs of testing while maintaining a high level of confidence in the final installation procedures.

Installation testing is of a different nature to other types of operational testing. It is concerned with demonstrating that all of the configuration items that make up an operational IT service have been installed correctly and that Computer Operations staff have all the resources they require to run the software to provide an IT service.

Once installation tests have been designed for a system, they are only likely to change if the system configuration changes.

3.1.8.1 Range of testing

The range of testing required may be substantial. The following headings may be useful as a checklist:

Functionality

All programs, on-line screens, outputs etc and the full range of hardware involved, should be invoked to show that they are present in the configuration and can be run.

Documentation

Check that all configuration items and their relationships are fully documented, and recorded in the configuration management database.

Operability

All the necessary operating instructions and procedures should be in place and work efficiently and be understood by the operators affected.

Job control language (JCL) suites

All JCL suites must be tested to show that all JCL libraries and procedures are present and can be run without error.

Parameter files

Many IT services require parameter files, and these should be checked to show that they have been set correctly for live running. A parameter file may simply store the current pay scales or VAT rates, or they may be used in a more complex manner to control the way in which programs update files, or extract information from databases.

Security and access

Tests may be required to show that all installed configuration items have the correct security and access permissions. With integrated systems, additional tests may be required to show that other IT services have the appropriate access to shared items such as database files. This work should be carried out in consultation with the IT security officer.

Database loading and data conversion

Where new databases are being created and loaded, tests may be required to show that loading has been successful, and that there are no data integrity problems. If existing data has to be converted to cope with enhancements to a database, then similar integrity tests may be required.

Hardware configuration

When software is designed to be installed on a range of hardware configurations, additional tests may be required for different configurations.

Rollback and recovery

Staff undertaking installation tests should look for cases where the installation procedures are unable to recover from error conditions. If operational software fails in use, the data files must be capable of being rolled back to a position where the data is accurate, and the IT service must be able to recover and proceed from that point onwards. Installation test staff should look for errors such as incomplete rollback, duplicate entries or inconsistent states.

3.1.8.2 Hardware and software resources required

The requirements for installation testing are generally similar to those described for system testing in section 3.1.7. Testers need to be able to test a wide enough range of configurations to engender confidence in the overall design

Section 3
Planning for operational test management

of the procedures. In some instances it may be necessary for installation testers to reconfigure hardware and software, and this may lead to system crashes. As with system testing, it is therefore recommended that installation testing is carried out on dedicated hardware, or out of business hours.

3.1.9 Developing procedures for acceptance testing

Acceptance testing procedures should:

* satisfy users and computer operations staff that the system as installed meets the contract conditions and/or acceptance test criteria such that the user is prepared to sign a system acceptance document (in many cases the acceptance test criteria will include demonstrating that an IT service will meet service level requirements)

* demonstrate that the software does not affect either the functions or service levels of other IT services

* enable customers to test their own procedures and to demonstrate that they are ready to use the new or amended IT service

* perform any outstanding tests which for practical reasons could not be completed in earlier test stages.

Often the signed acceptance document is the instrument authorizing either payment for the complete system or the release of a final stage payment. Any contract or test specification should state the requirements for acceptance. These may include statements of requirement covering functionality, load/stress, volume, configuration, conversion, security, performance, reliability, recovery, hardware maintenance, publications and human factors.

Clearly it is not desirable, or even feasible, to repeat all of the tests performed in earlier stages of development and acceptance which may also be included in an acceptance test specification. The design of system and installation tests can be used to perform many aspects of acceptance testing. It may be possible to provide documentary evidence that such tests have been successfully completed.

Acceptance tests should be specified and designed at the same time as other operational tests in order to ensure the specific objectives of the acceptance are achieved without duplication of effort between the different operational

The IT Infrastructure Library
Testing an IT Service for Operational Use

testing stages. Documentation of the acceptance tests should contain the conditions of acceptance relating to the IT service.

However, users may wish to run unscripted tests (ie without prior discussion with the supplier), and by this stage the IT service should be able to cope with any tests that users care to run. In addition, users may wish to run new tests in order to gain confidence in the IT service. It should be borne in mind however, that when components of an IT service, eg software, come from an external supplier, the basis for formal acceptance is established in the contract and the tests required should be anticipated. Notwithstanding the legal position, if 'new' tests are conceived after the contract requirements have been agreed, it is still of value for an organization to know before live running how an IT service will perform.

3.1.9.1 Involvement of customers

Acceptance testing is a formal process in which the service supplier and the user of a system are satisfying themselves that the conditions of any contract or acceptance test specification have been met. Those involved in the process should be drawn from all involved areas including:

* suppliers of the IT service, these may be external, internal or a combination of both (eg internal software suppliers combined with externally sourced hardware to provide a new service)

* business users, who authorize acceptance (the customer for the IT service)

* end-users who have the detailed knowledge of the business function to assess the IT service.

Usually the supplier and potential user are separate units, either totally separate organizations or different divisions within a single organization, and are regarded as such in the following discussion.

The supplier is familiar with the IT service and has confidence in its ability to meet the specified requirements, particularly if its development has been well controlled and few or no known errors remain on completion of the operational system and installation tests. In many ways the supplier is demonstrating the system rather than testing it. There is thus a tendency for suppliers to take the results of tests for granted and be motivated to complete the process as quickly as possible.

Section 3
Planning for operational test management

Users should, therefore, be fully aware that they are driving the acceptance testing stage, and that the IT service supplier should conform to *their* test requirements.

The difference in perspective between users and IT staff needs to be addressed. In particular, users should consider the following points to help them through acceptance testing:

* IT staff are not usually expert in day-to-day business practices, and will not necessarily know the subtleties of how the IT service is to be used to support business transactions

* users should consider whether tests proposed by the supplier are fully adequate, since they will have been derived from a knowledge of what the IT service can do, rather than from the users viewpoint of what the IT service *needs* to do

* users should be prepared to ask the supplier, at any time, for additional tests to be performed, and should take note if the supplier starts to raise any objections, since such objections could be based upon a lack of confidence in the IT service's ability to pass additional tests

* users should observe tests in detail and be prepared to ask questions, no matter how simple they appear to be

* users should not allow the supplier to give technical, jargon based, answers to questions - if the supplier cannot explain any unexpected results encountered during these tests in a way that users understand, then the problem should be referred back to the supplier.

Users may find it desirable to obtain expert assistance in the form of consultancy support. This could be obtained from external consultants or the organization's own IT Directorate, especially when the IT service is being developed elsewhere.

However, the main emphasis of acceptance testing should be focused on the need to demonstrate that, from the users' perspective, the IT service is fit for operational use.

Users should familiarize themselves with the functions and facilities of the IT service being tested before becoming involved in the actual test running. However, in reality, it is often the case that users are learning how to operate new IT services at the same time as performing tests on the system. This brings with it the danger that users may treat acceptance testing as a training course, thereby detracting from the quality of the testing.

If possible, a prototype or simulation of the final IT service should also be produced during requirements analysis. This can be a very useful training tool, serving as a living definition of what the software should do, and thereby facilitating usability testing.

3.1.9.2 Range of testing

In principle the range of testing may be the same as for system testing, except that acceptance tests are designed and executed by the users. In practice, however, it is usual for users to make an appropriate selection of tests. As stated earlier, users can satisfy themselves that the IT service is satisfactory either by asking the supplier for documentary evidence of performance as measured by the system tests, or (for changes to IT services) by including the running of regression tests as part of the test plan.

During acceptance tests much greater emphasis can be placed on testing whether the software meets service level requirements. System testing should have provided some indication of service level acceptability through tests on contributory elements such as performance and the reactions of the software to stress and volume. However system tests may not be able to test service levels fully, eg if a network is not available at that time.

3.1.9.3 Hardware and software resources required

Acceptance testing should be carried out in the operational environment with the IT service configuration to be used in normal working. Since the hardware is likely to be supporting other live IT services it is important that all affected staff, including users, help desk, operations and availability management, are made aware of and plan for:

* the possibility of system crashes

* any temporary requirement for the allocation of additional disk capacity, processing power or memory space to support the test requirements

* the need for out-of-hours system availability where testing is carried out outside normal operating hours to minimize disruption to the business

* any requirement for exclusive use of peripherals or other processing units.

A supplier running acceptance tests involving many users may require resources similar to those provided for system and installation testing.

3.1.10 Planning a pilot project

When planning to implement a revised operational testing function, it is advisable to commence with a pilot project, based upon a single software development or maintenance project, rather than introduce the new practices throughout the organization at one time. The advantages that this approach offers are:

* good management control over the first use of the testing procedures
* only limited resources, in terms of budget and staff, are required
* the ability to identify problems, and to modify the operational testing procedures quickly in order to resolve them
* a relatively quick evaluation of all aspects of the operational testing function
* a basis of confidence is established before proceeding to a wider implementation of the new operational testing procedures.

Only in the smallest organizations may it be feasible to implement operational testing without a pilot project.

3.1.10.1 Selection criteria for a pilot project

Care must be taken to choose a suitable pilot project. This may be a formal project introducing a new IT service or may be a maintenance project, enhancing an existing IT service. The ideal criteria for selecting a pilot project are that:

* it is a complete software project, including all software development stages
* it is a project which will be completed in a fairly short timescale of, say, 6 months or less
* all aspects of the operational testing function are required by the project

* the development project itself does not involve the use of new software technologies, eg new design methods, or programming languages that are being tried on an experimental basis

* the pilot project requires acceptable levels of operational testing resources, ie sufficient testing staff can be recruited and trained to support the project.

In practice, it may not be possible to meet all of these criteria. There may not be a development project starting at the right time which fulfils the requirements for a pilot. In this case it is necessary to determine the minimum set of criteria which should be met. The suggested minima are that the project:

* includes all software development stages

* will be completed within the 6 month guideline.

The reasons for recommending these particular criteria are:

* all stages of operational testing must be exercised, from test planning through to execution

* the results of the pilot project should be available in a short timescale in order to provide an early assessment of the operational testing function, and to enable full implementation of that function to be considered without undue delay.

The selection of a pilot project which only meets the minimum criteria involves additional risks, and places a greater burden on the Operational Test Manager when assessing the effectiveness of the revised operational testing function. For example if a pilot project is chosen where new software development methods and/or languages are being used, the inevitable problems associated with unfamiliarity may well inhibit objective assessment of the new operational testing practices.

Where possible, the staff involved in producing the software should be sympathetic to the introduction of the testing function. If there is antipathy to the testing proposals, this could well result in a lack of co-operation during the pilot which may in turn damage the longer term prospects of introducing the new function throughout the organization.

Section 3
Planning for operational test management

3.1.10.2 The pilot project test plan

It is necessary to develop a test plan for the pilot project. It is recommended that this plan should include the following steps:

* establish the objectives of the test plan, and determine the measures required to show whether the objectives are being met

* estimate the resources required to support the test plan

* recruit and train the staff required to implement the pilot project

* arrange for the installation of supporting computer systems

* build the test environment, which includes implementing and checking software tools

* modify the proposed operational testing procedures to meet the pilot project's requirements

* develop a test schedule which is integrated with the development plan

* define the management reporting required and the main review points within the project

* conduct a project evaluation review of the pilot and assess the results against the original objectives.

3.1.11 Expansion of the operational testing function

From the project evaluation review of the pilot project, decisions may be taken on the expansion of the operational testing function. The major planning considerations are:

* finalize any changes to the function in the light of experience from the pilot project

* identify workloads and produce initial work schedules in consultation with the development managers; decisions need to be made about bringing ongoing software development and maintenance projects in line with the new IT service

The IT Infrastructure Library
Testing an IT Service for Operational Use

* set up a database to collect key quality measures, this data may already be available from the configuration management or other service management databases (see section 3.1.3.1); this data will enable periodic reports to be produced for post-implementation monitoring of the operational testing function (see section 5)

* ensure that all the required software tools and/or automated test facilities have been obtained, installed and tested

* re-allocate (or recruit) and train staff needed for full implementation of operational testing

* determine the audit, and review the schedule, required to monitor full implementation of the operational testing function.

If the operational testing function is going to be applied to existing IT services which are under maintenance, then additional issues need to be considered:

* whether any existing test environments can be adopted and modified as required by the operational testing function

* whether operational testing is to be applied to all or part of the IT services

* how test procedures are to be applied

* contractual arrangements.

3.1.12 Management information and measurement

It is essential to plan for the provision of management information, and supporting measures, which are required to help control the testing function.

The most important management reports are those required to control the test operation. Reports should be raised for each development project using a standard format, and they can then be consolidated into an overall report. These reports may contain information about:

* project progress against the schedule

* actual versus estimated costs

* the number of test runs performed

Section 3
Planning for operational test management

* the number of errors found
* the current status of configuration items under test
* any problems during the reporting period
* anticipated problems, eg where project progress indicates that there will be slippage.

Reports of differing levels of detail may be produced at different intervals. For example, there may be monthly summary reports on each project for use internally by the Operational Test Manager, and summary monthly reports which are used to produce a consolidated external report for senior management.

The effectiveness of the management reporting should be monitored. Some of the questions that can be raised are:

* do the reports enable management to exercise control over testing work?
* is the information in the reports both valuable and easy to assimilate?
* is there any redundant or missing information?
* are reports produced in good time?
* do reports require an acceptable level of management time to produce?
* are there any suggested improvements?

3.2 Dependencies

Successful planning depends on the commitment of IT directors and senior managers to improving the quality of delivered IT services. The results of the impact and cost/benefit analyses can help by facilitating an investigation into current practice and the possibilities for improvement.

There are other dependencies which may affect planning:

* the availability of a suitable software development or maintenance project to act as a pilot
* the efficiency and effectiveness of other IT service management functions which interface with operational testing, eg:
    - service level management
    - capacity management

The IT Infrastructure Library
Testing an IT Service for Operational Use

- problem management
- software control and distribution
- change management

* the co-operation of software developers and maintainers, users, external suppliers etc (the IT Infrastructure Library modules **Customer Liaison** and **Managing Supplier Relationships** refer).

3.3 People

The success of any function within IT Services rests ultimately upon the skills, experience and attitude of the people involved; management, staff and customers. This is equally true of operational testing, where traditionally testing has been an unattractive area of work for skilled and experienced staff. This situation is changing, as there has been considerable development of testing both as a software discipline, and as an important element in reducing the risks of operational errors.

Management must be aware of the potential business benefits of testing, and 'sell' the attractions accordingly. In particular the importance to the organization of good operational testing procedures should be emphasized and the wide view of IT and business environments that is required for, and available to, staff working in the operational testing function.

3.3.1 Organization

The position of operational testing within the organization provides a direct measure of the importance attached to software quality by the senior management. The main requirement is that operational testing should be independent of development and maintenance, both in its management structure and in its resources. There are a number of ways in which operational testing can be integrated within an organization:

* as a separate operational testing function
* with operational testing specialists attached to individual projects
* operational testing incorporated as a component of quality assurance
* operational testing implemented by functional user departments.

Section 3
Planning for operational test management

The importance of the operational testing function should not be under-rated. Its budget often accounts for up to 50% of the cost of software development projects (source, the CAST Report).

There may be many roles in an operational testing group, and also many ways in which an organization may wish to organize testing staff in order to meet the demands of specific software development and maintenance projects.

Figure 3 gives an example of operational testing roles and how they may be structured (see section 3.3.3 for further information on testing roles).

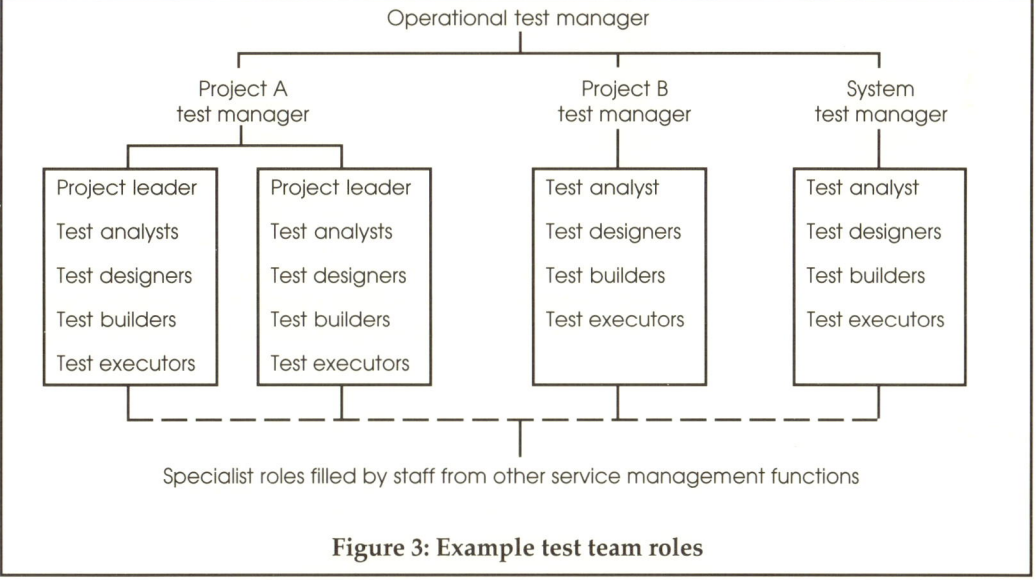

Figure 3: Example test team roles

In the example, three of the possible test team structures are shown:

* a large project, project A, which requires more than one testing team, where each test team could be responsible for all aspects of operational testing for a particular phase or part of the project

* a smaller project with a single team responsible for all operational testing, where there may be a single test manager or a project leader responsible for the project

* a test team which specializes in system testing, but which can service more than one project.

The IT Infrastructure Library
Testing an IT Service for Operational Use

Figure 3 shows a link between test teams and other service management functions, to indicate that there are specialist roles where staff from other IT service management functions may need to be co-opted onto an operational test team. Section 3.3.6 illustrates the involvement of other IT service management functions in more detail.

Apart from the internal operational testing roles and their structure, there will be very strong links between the operational testing function and the users. This is discussed in section 3.3.5. In summary, whilst users have the responsibility to perform acceptance testing, it has to be acknowledged that, in most cases, users are not trained in testing techniques. Therefore the operational testing function should aim to provide staff to guide users on all aspects of acceptance testing, from defining test requirements, through test design to test running.

3.3.2 Operational Test Manager

The main responsibilities of the Operational Test Manager have been listed in section 3.1.1. From this list it can be deduced that the person appointed should:

* have good interpersonal skills with the ability to relate to managers, technical staff and users at all levels

* have the respect of both users and IT staff

* understand the organization's business objectives

* be able to communicate well both orally and in writing

* understand all aspects of testing.

A person with such skills may have a background in IT development or services, but could equally well come from a user department having a heavy involvement with computerized systems.

3.3.3 Testing roles

The following is a list of the roles which may be required in a testing group:

* test managers, responsible for planning and implementing system testing during a development project

Section 3
Planning for operational test management

* test analysts, who can analyze the requirement for testing and assess the resources required
* test designers, who can design test suites and write test plans
* test builders, who can write the test cases required in test suites
* test executors, who can run tests, and document and analyze the results
* support personnel to ensure the orderly keeping of records and who maintain administrative links with development, change management, configuration management and with the project quality assurance team.

Given the range of operational testing there may be scope within large organizations for the development of specialist skills in particular testing areas. Possible specialist areas would include:

* configuration testing
* security testing (possibly the responsibility of the IT security officer)
* usability and other human factors
* documentation.

If beta site testing, pilot running or parallel running are employed then non-specialist staff may be required to supervise the running and collation of results from tests run by users.

In a smaller organization a single person may perform more than one operational testing function. For example a test analyst might also be a designer and builder as well, particularly upon a single major development or maintenance project. Such organizations will not have the option to develop the staff specialisms described above, but will need to rely on the skills of fewer people to ensure that the range of tests is adequately covered.

3.3.4 Testing skills

The skills required in a test group will vary depending on the circumstances. Some examples of the skills are shown below.

An IT background — This may be in the design, programming or maintenance of software, or in running or using software on a range of hardware.

The IT Infrastructure Library
Testing an IT Service for Operational Use

A sceptical approach	A tester should not accept *on-faith* anything claimed about a program's functions or operation. The tester has to translate such claims into testable assertions, and demonstrate whether or not the claims are true.
Insight and perception	For example a user may report a problem which appears to have been missed during testing. Why was the problem overlooked and is it a new type of problem? Is it necessary to develop new test cases which will find problems of this type?
Intuition	Any test plan may have limitations in the test coverage it provides - the intuitive tester can spot weaknesses in a plan, and run additional tests which may then reveal a problem.
Communication skills	Most test reports, whether written or verbal, describe problems or software errors, and therefore it is essential that test staff can express their findings accurately and completely. Test staff should be able to document factually and objectively what has happened during test runs, so that other staff do not perceive test reports as a threat, eg test reports should not seek to allocate blame for a software error.
Observation	Able to concentrate on detail, and with the patience not to overlook indications of problems.
Empathy	Test staff should be able to imagine how users will operate an application, and ask the question "how could I get in trouble here if I had never used a computer before?"

For installation testing, staff may require additional skills relating to the:

* configuration of hardware
* operating system functions.

For acceptance testing, the following additional skills are required:

* the ability to work with users, user management, operations staff and support staff; staff who may be particularly suitable are business and systems analysts, and others with applications oriented experience
* the ability to run predefined tests in the presence of the supplier
* the ability to record results accurately and liaise with the supplier to ensure that problems are resolved

Section 3
Planning for operational test management

* the ability to prioritize the requirements of the organization so that high priority items can be checked first.

3.3.5 Involvement of users

The involvement of users should be carefully co-ordinated and monitored so that users have the opportunity to use their own skills and experience to add value to operational testing. Users are ideally placed to provide positive feedback to the development process and become enthusiastic ambassadors for the IT service under test. Their input and advice can be sought on any aspect but is likely to be most helpful in the areas of functionality, performance, user documentation and human factors.

Users are the final arbiters on the success or failure of operational testing. The testing function provides a service to the users, since they will need the skills of testing staff to help them in this work. For example, if users wish to test the performance and capacity of an IT service under heavy load conditions, then they may require technical support in designing and running such tests.

3.3.6 Involvement of other IT service management staff

A system test group will require support from other IT service management functions. Other modules in the IT Infrastructure Library describe how these functions should be set up and run. The functions which need to be involved are:

* service level and availability management, to determine the tests that are needed to show whether an IT service will meet service level requirements

* computer operations management, to define operability requirements, and then assess whether the IT service meets them

* capacity management, to plan the capacity needs of new and revised IT services, and then monitor actual IT capacity used during operational testing

* configuration and change management, to control the movement of software and hardware through the testing stages

* software control and distribution, to control the release of software for operational running

57

The IT Infrastructure Library
Testing an IT Service for Operational Use

* problem management, to assist in recording and tracking problems during operational testing

* Help Desk, to assess whether the correct information is available for the Help Desk to support the new or revised IT service

* cost management, to monitor the costs of operational testing

* quality management, to ensure that testing work is performed according to the project quality plan and the quality management system.

3.3.7 Staffing levels required

The number of staff required to plan and implement operational testing for a software development or maintenance project will depend upon the following factors:

* level of confidence of the testing function in the quality of the developed IT service and in the testing already performed during development

* degree of importance of the software, i.e. its criticality to the business

* size and complexity of the IT service under test

* test coverage required

* degree of automation possible

* nature and type of test management tools installed.

Until experience is gained of using these factors to estimate the number of staff required for operational testing, organizations should use simple algorithms for planning the number of test staff. One method is to assume firstly that operational testing takes a certain percentage of the total development effort, eg 40%, and that system testing in turn consumes a percentage of the operational test effort, eg 60% of 40%. Such a crude approach will necessarily prove inaccurate but can offer a starting point to which experience can then be applied.

3.3.8 Training and awareness

Training courses on various aspects of testing are available from several consultancies and training organizations. It is not practical to be specific since courses can change rapidly in content and availability.

Section 3
Planning for operational test management

Training needs to be tailored and targeted to the differing individual and skill levels involved with the operational testing function. For example, users need training in acceptance testing. Managers need to be aware of the basic purpose of testing, how it relates to quality, what they can expect from operational testing functions, the limitations of testing, and what economic constraints they need to apply to testing activities to get the most cost-effective testing.

All software development and maintenance staff should be trained in basic testing techniques, since they are very effective at improving the quality of software produced. All software development managers should be trained in the management of testing.

Specialist testers from the operational testing group need more detailed training, and also involvement in keeping up with the state of the art in their specialized field, including access to books and journals, special interest groups, seminars and conferences. In summary, testing should be included in any organization's training and education plans for the professional development of its IT staff.

3.4 Timing

The results of operational testing form the basis upon which the quality of IT services are assessed, therefore the sooner operational testing is applied to projects the earlier that benefits are realized.

The amount of time required to complete the planning stage of the operational testing function depends upon the following factors:

* size and complexity of installed and planned IT services
* the balance between packaged and bespoke software
* the balance between in-house and sub-contract development
* the experience of the staff involved.

It is necessary to plan well ahead of the need to test IT services, so that all functions of the testing service are in place, resourced and ready to operate according to schedule.

The IT Infrastructure Library
Testing an IT Service for Operational Use

Section 4
Implementing operational testing

4. Implementing operational testing

The implementation phase of operational testing involves executing the plans determined in section 3. Whilst every care should have been taken to anticipate problems during the planning stages, some concerns will inevitably arise during implementation.

4.1 Procedures

Procedures are described in two categories:

* as applied to a pilot project
* for development of an ongoing service.

4.1.1 Pilot testing project

4.1.1.1 Resources and responsibilities

A successful pilot project depends on the correct resources being made available at the required time. For example it is necessary to ensure that staff have been allocated to the test group and have received training before testing begins. The responsibilities and job definitions should be agreed and publicized.

Other resources required include computer facilities and testing tools. It is necessary to ensure that the computer resources specified in the pilot project plan are made available. Furthermore, any testing tools should be installed, and training on their use completed before test work commences.

4.1.1.2 Test methods, standards and procedures

It is likely that during the pilot project the methods, standards and procedures developed in the planning stage will need modification and refinement in the light of experience. Reasons might include factors such as:

* the testing methods used to specify and design tests may require revision to be compatible with, say, new development techniques; eg more general test design methods may need modification to work with a particular development method such as SSADM

* testing standards need to be strengthened to ensure an acceptable degree of test coverage; eg a development project may embrace some new form of processing which is not covered by existing standards

* test procedures are found to be inefficient or difficult to adhere to, eg the procedure for dealing with software that fails tests should incorporate a decision process for determining whether all testing should stop, or whether limited testing can continue; if testing is stopped prematurely then the length of the testing stages may be significantly extended.

4.1.1.3 Test management

The management of test suites, by which is meant all test specifications, designs, test cases, test data and test jobs, may be quite a complex task. Monitoring should be put in place to ensure the integrity of all the data and information retained for operational testing purposes.

In particular it should be established as early during the pilot as possible that tests designed to be incorporated into regression packs can be used for this purpose. During the pilot project, several versions of the tested software may be created as errors are corrected and new versions re-submitted for testing. When a new version is produced, there is an opportunity for regression test packs to be updated, and test runs made to demonstrate their maintainability.

4.1.1.4 Scope of testing

In section 3, the three main stages of operational testing were described, and the scope of each stage discussed in detail. It was stressed that there are not fixed boundaries between these stages. For example performance tests which should ideally be run during system testing may have to wait until acceptance testing if the necessary hardware is not available at the earlier stage.

Consequently, the scope of each testing stage should be monitored to ensure that test runs are performed during the stage when their results will be valid.

Section 4
Implementing operational testing

4.1.1.5 General testing effectiveness

In addition to the specific issues described above for the pilot project, the general effectiveness of operational testing needs to be monitored throughout the pilot in order to identify and resolve any problems which adversely affect test quality and cost-effectiveness.

For example tests which are effective at finding errors, may require significant effort and expense to specify, design and implement. During implementation it is vital to ensure that test suites are designed to be maintainable, otherwise there will be continual overheads associated with test re-creation. Lessons learnt from the pilot project should provide input to others on how to develop good tests.

Other potential issues include:

* test tools which fail to deliver the expected benefits
* under-estimation of the size and complexity of testing work
* conflicts in the use of resources.

Plans should be amended to reflect solutions to such problems found during the pilot.

4.1.1.6 Financial monitoring

Although with experience it is possible to estimate the costs of the testing relating to a proposed system or change, it is only when the system has passed its final tests and has been released that all the costs will be known. However, it is not usually acceptable to wait until the end of a project to report a large cost overrun.

During the pilot project, testing costs should be monitored and forecasts made in management reports of expected final costs. Costs may be estimated initially when test plans are developed, and refined as testing proceeds.

4.1.2 Ongoing implementation

4.1.2.1 Resources and responsibilities

Successful implementation of operational testing on an ongoing basis depends on additional resources being made available at the required times to support development or maintenance projects. The experience gained from recruiting and training staff for the pilot project should be used to refine the recruitment procedure, and to improve the effectiveness of training. As the testing group takes on more work, it may be necessary to identify new responsibilities, and to revise job definitions.

The other resources required, such as computer facilities and testing tools, may need to be enhanced to meet the test requirements of more projects. It is necessary to ensure that growth of these resources is specified in the implementation plan.

4.1.2.2 Test methods, standards and procedures

The pilot project should have refined the methods, standards and procedures to some degree. As more projects start, it is necessary to continue this process of refinement so that these methods, standards and procedures are developed to meet the needs of many projects.

4.1.2.3 Test management

As the testing function takes on more work, the control of test suites may become an increasing management problem. Whilst the pilot project should have shown that the initial test management system is effective, the inclusion of new projects may place additional demands on the operational testing function. Therefore it is necessary to continue refining the procedures to ensure that operational testing continues to work correctly.

4.1.2.4 Scope of testing

In section 3, the scope of testing was described for each stage. During ongoing implementation this will require revision to ensure that for a specific development or maintenance project:

* the scope of each testing stage is correct, that is certain tests may need to be moved from one stage to another

* additional tests are added, or unnecessary ones removed, according to the test requirements.

4.1.2.5 General testing effectiveness

The task of assessing testing effectiveness which started in the pilot project needs to be continued during ongoing implementation.

Section 4
Implementing operational testing

Whilst the approach suggested in 4.1.1.5 applies to ongoing projects, as experience is accumulated it should be possible to make more objective assessments. For example, as the operational history of the IT service is extended, more information will be accumulated concerning errors which were found during live running rather than in operational testing. This information can highlight any weaknesses in operational testing, and enable improvements to be made to increase testing effectiveness.

4.1.2.6 Forecasting testing workloads

Where testing is taking place on a computer on which live IT services run, service levels may be affected by certain testing activities. This situation should be recognized during test planning, and agreement obtained with users for a temporary reduction in service levels.

Forecasts should be made during ongoing implementation of future testing workloads, so that the Operational Test Manager can highlight such activities and forewarn other IT service management functions such as computer operations and service level management. Together they can make suitable arrangements to minimize the impact on users. This might include scheduling tests to run at night, weekends, or holidays, or warning users that a reduced level of service can be expected for the duration of the tests.

4.1.2.7 Financial monitoring

Some initial experience of financial monitoring will have been gained during the pilot project. This experience, plus that gained from ongoing projects, should be used to refine the estimating methods.

As more projects are completed, it should be possible to analyze how the variance between estimated and actual costs has changed over time.

4.2 Dependencies

The implementation plan for operational testing should be integrated with software development project plans, so that the operational testing function can provide the right services at the right time during development. However, development projects frequently suffer from slippage, and this can have significant effects on operational testing in several ways.

Firstly it is essential to ensure that schedules revised as a result of slippage allow sufficient time for testing work. If development schedules slip this must not be allowed to reduce the time allocated for test running. Consider the reasons why development projects are late. It may be that if analysts and programmers are under pressure to complete their work this may result in more errors and a greater need for testing. In this case a better solution may be to revise release dates for the finished IT service.

Secondly, any revision in timescales may affect the ability of the operational testing function to resource a particular test plan. It is unlikely that the overall operational testing plan will contain much slack time. Consequently if testing staff are not able to complete work on one project at the time agreed, it may have to remain unfinished as the staff are required to work on other projects. This is an unsatisfactory situation, but one which needs to be resolved with project managers.

Prior to an operational testing function being implemented the configuration and change management functions should be in place, since these functions identify and control the status of the IT service under test. Without these functions, the operational testing cannot demonstrate that the version of software and documentation tested is that which is subsequently released for live running.

4.3 People

During the implementation of both the pilot and ongoing projects it is necessary to monitor the organization, roles and effectiveness of testing staff. As new test groups are created, their planned structures and the roles within them may require modification as projects progress. Section 6.3 describes in more detail the people-related problems which may be encountered.

4.4 Timing

It is impossible to give specific guidelines on the length of time that might be required to implement the function, nor the most appropriate point in time for an organization to do so. The number of variables involved is far too great. However some of the major factors are:

* the availability of a project to act as a pilot

* the size of new IT services being developed

Section 4
Implementing operational testing

* organizational pressures to implement operational testing for existing IT services which suffer from poor software quality
* the time required to recruit and train staff
* the time required to search for, evaluate and implement testing tools
* whether other IT service management functions are available when needed to support a test plan.

The IT Infrastructure Library
Testing an IT Service for Operational Use

Section 5
Post-implementation and audit

5. Post-implementation and audit

Once the revised operational testing function has been implemented, a Project Evaluation Review (PER) should be carried out. This will review the project against such parameters as timescale and resource usage.

When sufficient time has elapsed to assess the success (or otherwise) of the project, as measured against the declared objectives, a Post-Implementation Review (PIR) should take place. In the longer term, there will be a need for regular efficiency and effectiveness reviews of the function as part of the ongoing management of the operational testing function.

It is worth emphasizing that the PER and PIR referred to above apply to the implementation of the entire operational testing function itself. There will be a PER and PIR carried out for each of the software development and maintenance projects taking place within an organization. Each of these projects will have been subject to operational testing and thus the reviews will assist the managers of the operational testing function to review the efficiency, effectiveness and economy of their function.

Consequently, this section is concerned primarily with PER, PIR and audit reviews of:

* the pilot project
* the operational testing function.

5.1 Procedures

Whether the PIR is performed for a pilot project or an ongoing operational testing function, it is recommended that an agreed set of procedures be used, since the information which needs to be considered is similar for both. It is only the possible outcomes of the PIRs that may differ. For example, the PIR of a pilot project could lead to a decision to bring forward plans for implementing an independent operational testing service. By comparison the PIR of an ongoing service is more likely to reach decisions about improving effectiveness and productivity.

The following procedures may be applied to the PIR of either a pilot project or the operational testing function. They cover two main topics:

* determining how well the operational testing function is meeting its objectives

The IT Infrastructure Library
Testing an IT Service for Operational Use

* reviewing the issues and problems which have arisen during implementation and identifying changes which need to made.

5.1.1 Reviewing objectives

Reviewing the success of the operational testing function at meeting its objectives consists of two parts:

* assessing whether the objectives remain valid following the implementation of the operational testing function

* analyzing which objectives have been met, and to what degree, and understanding why objectives were not met and what lessons can be learnt.

To achieve this it is necessary to have defined measurable objectives, and to have the means of measuring them (see section 3.1.12). Typical objectives are to:

* implement the operational testing function within a specified budget, and agreed schedules and resources

* demonstrate that IT services released to the live environment meet minimum reliability requirements

* achieve a certain level of testing efficiency, eg measure the number of test cases required to find an error

* achieve set levels of test coverage, eg the number of types of test case per transaction

* achieve a cost/justifiable balance between the effort expended on test planning and design, and that on test running.

To support these objectives a number of performance measures will be required, and they include:

* the numbers and types of errors found during each test run, and the duration of the test run

* rates at which errors were found and fixed during the operational testing stages

* the number and types of errors found in live running which were not detected during the software development lifecycle

Section 5
Post-implementation and audit

* time recording details which give the effort expended on
  - every test activity in each operational testing stage
  - individual test runs
* variances between estimates of operational testing work and the actual figures
* the costs of computer resources used.

The review should consider reasons not only for situations where objectives are not met, but also where they are met or even exceeded. This will lead to an understanding of the factors that affect the performance of the operational testing function.

Where the operational testing function is successful, the reasons should be analyzed, so that this success can be repeated in the future. Where objectives are not met it will be necessary to distinguish between those which were genuinely over-ambitious, and those where failure was due to poor implementation.

5.1.2 Reviewing issues and problems

During implementation, many issues and problems are likely to arise. Whilst some will be minor, and may be resolved immediately, others may not be. All of them, save for the most trivial, should be recorded in the project file.

The Operational Test Manager will need to classify the problems so that they can be dealt with in the correct way. Problems may relate to the following areas:

* project management, planning and estimation
* personnel
* organization
* communications with others
* test methods, standards and procedures
* hardware and software resources, including testing tools
* support from other IT service management functions.

71

In all cases some form of resolution should be found, and problems should not be left unresolved.

In order to review all of this information in a satisfactory way, the Operational Test Manager will need to adopt some structure to the review process. It is recommended that a review contains the following tasks:

* an internal management review, to consider all issues relating to overall operational testing effectiveness

* an external review with users to consider their views on the role and effectiveness of the operational testing function

* an operational testing staff review, where testers can raise and discuss issues

* if required, more detailed reviews to deal with specific management or technical problems which have been identified.

Following these reviews, attention should be given to the way in which improvement actions are implemented. The implementation of changes or improvements to the operational testing function may have a significant impact for ongoing operational testing work, and therefore this should not be done in an *ad hoc* way. The Operational Test Manager should maintain a separate improvement plan. As PIRs take place, so any new items can be added to the improvement plan and scheduled for implementation.

5.1.3 Audits

Audits should be carried out in accordance with any quality management system (QMS) being used by the organization. It is beyond the scope of this module to discuss the details of a QMS, and reference should be made to the Quality Library module on **Quality Audit** and the IT Infrastructure Library module **Quality Management for IT Services**.

The main purpose of audits are to:

* check that operational testing work is being performed in accordance with the organization's quality plan (which may be based on a standard such as ISO9001/EN29001/BS5750 Part 1) and documented procedures

* ensure that appropriate records and audit trails are being maintained for all configuration items

* analyze trends and identify improvements.

Section 5
Post-implementation and audit

5.2 Dependencies

The long term success of an operational testing function depends on being able to demonstrate its effectiveness and efficiency to:

* users and user managers
* software development and maintenance groups
* the IT director or equivalent board-level manager.

This should include a commitment to improve the operational testing function as a cost-effective IT function which contributes to the production of IT services conforming to the organization's stated requirements.

5.3 People

PIRs may be performed either by the Operational Test Manager or a consultant (internal or external).

There will be a need to invite staff from other groups within the organization to contribute to the PIR. For example:

* users, who play a major part in acceptance testing, will need to express their views as to how well the function is performing, and how well it supports the users
* software development and maintenance managers should be asked to contribute their views, particularly on the way in which operational test personnel work and communicate with their own staff
* staff from the other IT service management functions who are involved at various stages of operational testing should provide representatives who can comment on the effectiveness of their involvement.

The personnel responsible for audits should be specified by the organization's QMS. In organizations with a certified QMS, eg to ISO9001 standards, formally trained and qualified quality auditors will be required.

5.4 Timing

The PER of the operational testing function should take place following implementation, probably at or about the same time as the PIR of the pilot project. The PIR of the operational testing function should normally be held between 6 and 12 months after the new procedures are implemented, the precise timing will depend upon the

The IT Infrastructure Library
Testing an IT Service for Operational Use

timescale of projects being subject to operational testing since it is pointless to hold the PIR until sufficient information has accrued to make it a worthwhile exercise.

Ongoing audits to assess the efficiency and effectiveness of the operational testing function might take place:

* in conjunction with the PIR of a software development project

* on a periodic basis, eg six monthly or annually

* after a major piece of software maintenance work has been completed.

Section 6
Benefits, costs and possible problems

6. Benefits, costs and possible problems

6.1 Benefits

Operational testing is an essential element of any quality assurance programme, eg see ISO9000-3, section 5.7. Without an operational testing function, effective quality management is not possible. The benefits are:

* demonstrable fitness of an IT service for operational use

* reduced risk of operational software errors which lead to the major types of problems identified during gap analysis (see section 3.1.3.3)

* IT services which can meet agreed service levels

* the preservation of quality in existing IT services

* reduced costs of setting up tests since the overall testing strategy is in place which defines the procedures to be followed

* reduced costs of corrective maintenance

* reduced costs of running operational IT services

* higher user confidence in the provision of IT services

* improved reputation for the IT Directorate

* more reliable IT services will reduce the number of changes and releases and the risks associated with the distribution of new releases throughout the IT infrastructure (this can be highly significant for distributed IT systems).

From the quality management viewpoint, operational testing provides the means for users of IT services to validate acceptability according to previously agreed criteria.

One of the most important benefits resulting from the approach to operational testing described in this module is that the operational testing function will be tailored to the needs of the business. This should ensure that valuable testing resources are not wasted on irrelevant test work, but instead are focused on reducing those risks which most affect an organization.

6.2 Costs

The initial costs of setting up an operational testing function or of improving existing facilities may be substantial. The major cost elements will be:

* staff costs, noting that many test activities such as test analysis and design work are skilled, labour intensive tasks

* computer resources, as test running can require large amounts of both storage capacity and processing power

* maintenance of test suites and documentation, noting that the volume of testing material may become large, but that test suites should be seen as an investment - if they are not maintained then they may have to be redeveloped from scratch, a far more costly option

* licensing costs of tools, the full cost of ownership should be obtained including any maintenance or update charges; this could be substantial for tools which run on mainframes.

However, these costs have to be weighed against the benefits.

It will not be possible to measure the actual costs and benefits until the operational testing function has been running for a while. It would, therefore, be imprudent to make a very large initial investment at a time when the benefits were not certain. However, an organization should be able to make an informed guess at likely costs.

This is a powerful argument for adopting an incremental approach to implementation, through the use of pilot projects, which will considerably help management to control costs whilst assessing benefits.

If operational testing is performed manually then costs will be high and test effectiveness low. The use of automation and testing tools is therefore an essential factor in ultimately reducing costs through efficient use of staff.

Section 6
Benefits, costs and possible problems

6.3 Possible problems

There are a number of possible problems which may arise when implementing an operational testing function into an organization, including:

* an independent operational test function may generate adverse reactions from developers and maintainers

* the existence of the operational testing function could result in software developers and maintainers taking the view that they can abrogate some of their own testing responsibilities, eg programmers may think that because there is an operational testing section, they need not spend much time on unit and link testing

* the awareness campaign may fail in its efforts to win the support of IT staff

* objectives, if not clearly defined, cannot be measured against

* operational testing may be viewed as an intrusive critic's activity

* insensitive use of powers to reject software may lead to poor co-operation between operational testing and other IT groups

* a lack of support tools leads to inefficient and costly testing.

In section 3.0, some of the inherent conceptual problems of testing were described. In particular, attention was drawn to the fact that it is not possible to test systems fully. Issues which need to be considered are:

* existing systems may not be amenable to operational testing if their design is poor, in which case effort should not be wasted trying to test the untestable; in these circumstances more appropriate solutions to the problem may be redevelopment or re-engineering

* existing test suites may be both costly to run and inefficient in their ability to find errors; however, to embark on a complete redesign of tests may be an expensive and risky tactic; it may be better to consider automating the existing tests to reduce staff costs in the short term, and then to redesign incrementally.

Testing has often been viewed as a boring task, and as a result many IT staff prefer not to do it. Therefore, staff motivation is an issue that must be addressed from the outset. Possible solutions are to ensure that:

* all IT staff and users understand the essential value of operational testing to the business

* testing staff are recruited who have the desire and skills required for test work, and that staff are given professional training

* feedback is given to staff so that they are able to learn more about the effects of good and bad development practices on software quality, and are able to develop their own skills in these areas

* skilled testing staff are given challenging opportunities which use their skills, and that the boring aspects of testing are automated.

Where in-house software development and/or software maintenance units do not adopt a structured methods approach, it will be difficult to 'sell' the benefits of a structured approach to testing. The use of a structured approach to software development, eg SSADM, will aid operational testing in that logical design imposes a particular and consistent structure on required functions (which will have been detailed in the requirements catalogue). These functions are then translated into programs, thus the logical structure of specific programs is made visible in non-programmer terms, providing an understandable set of targets against which to test. Where the software development process does not produce these features, the operational testing role will incur extra overheads.

Finally, there is the problem of being over ambitious or over elaborate. A theme which runs through this module is the need to implement the function in a controlled way, preferably through the use of pilot projects. This applies at all times, not only during initial implementation. For example, if an opportunity is found to introduce automation, the tools should be used initially in an appropriate pilot scheme.

This list of possible problems is longer than the list of benefits given in section 6.1. This should not, however, be taken as an indication that implementing an operational testing function is a high risk endeavour to be avoided. These risks are all avoidable, and with a good proactive approach from management, the benefits can be accrued whilst avoiding the problems outlined.

7. Tools

7.1 Introduction

It has been emphasized that the use of tools may be a key factor in the successful implementation of an operational testing function. Therefore automation should be considered from the outset, even though the use of tools may not be possible in the early stages.

The reason for this is that the principle 'methods first and tools second' applies here just as it does in other areas of (software) engineering. This means that sound testing methods and practices should be established first, and then a review made of the opportunities for automation.

Whilst there are many types of tools available for software program testing, there are far fewer available for operational testing. This is due in part to the problems of trying to automate aspects of validation.

The main classes of tools for operational testing are:

* administrative tools, for the management and control of testing

* test run support tools, for automating test preparation, execution and maintenance

* special utilities, such as database integrity checkers and performance analyzers.

The following is a description of tool types that should be considered in each class.

For an Operational Test Manager developing a new function, the descriptions aim to give an *aide-mémoire* of the areas of automation that should be considered.

7.2 Administrative tools

Tools in this class can be considered for the following purposes.

Planning

Used for the production and maintenance of test plans, these include documentation, project management, estimating and budgetary control tools. Many organizations use PC-based tools for this type of work, and there are a large number from which to choose.

The IT Infrastructure Library
Testing an IT Service for Operational Use

Test design

Test suite design tools help in developing structured test cycles and the test cases which constitute each cycle. Different levels of tool sophistication may be applied to test design. At the simplest level, documentation tools may be used to prepare the designs on a purely textual basis. However organizations should consider using the analysis and design capabilities of any Computer Aided Software Engineering (CASE) tools they have adopted. CASE tools offer the advantages of developing links between information items, and this can provide additional integrity to test designs.

Error analysis

These comprise error recording, tracking and analysis tools. This is a key area for automation as the information is a primary output of the testing process. To enable this information to deliver maximum benefit, it is recommended that a database management system is used to control the recording. This will also permit a variety of management reports and analyses to be produced. Some of the widely used PC database tools should be considered.

Configuration management

Keeping test designs in step with software releases is a vital element in successful testing and will require the maintenance and control of test data and regression packs. Organizations with CM systems in place may be able to set up test sets and documentation as configuration items. Alternatively, it may be necessary to ensure that all test files have identifiers which link them to specific software releases.

7.3 Test run support tools

The tools in this class probably represent the greatest opportunity for improving testing productivity. The main tool types to be considered are given below.

Test schedulers

These provide testers with a means of selecting which test cycles to run, and then executing the tests with the minimum of manual intervention. Such tools will probably be based upon the job control facilities offered by the operating system which is used for testing.

Section 7
Tools

Schedulers can offer a number of functions which include:

* copying files to set up specific test environments
* construction of run jobs for the chosen test cycles
* invocation of tools for comparing test results with nominated master results sets
* cleaning up the test environment after testing.

Record and playback tools

Running tests on interactive systems can be labour intensive. Record and playback tools allow testers to mimic operators' responses automatically. Testers input test cycles and cases once, and if the results are successful, the input and output scripts can be recorded, and then replayed as and when required. Furthermore, the tools may allow editing of scripts, so that changes to test cycles can be made to account for IT service changes, or where test cycles require enhancement for new test cases.

File comparators

The ability to compare actual test results with master sets in an efficient and accurate way is one that should not rely on manual effort. Indeed, for systems with large databases, automatic file comparison may be essential. A key attribute of any file comparator is the degree of 'intelligence' it uses when comparing two files. For example, it is not considered acceptable for a comparator simply to discover a difference which puts the files out of step with each other and then report every remaining entry as a difference. Intelligent comparators can look ahead and attempt to re-synchronize files. Good comparators should offer testers a number of options in the look ahead facility, the way that certain types of mismatch are handled, and whether certain records are to be excluded from the comparison.

7.4 Specialist tools

This classification includes tools which are either not specifically considered as test tools, or which have to be produced by bespoke development to meet specific requirements.

Performance analyzers are one example, as these tools are usually in the domain of technical support or systems programming staff, and may be used for many reasons. Their contribution to operational testing is mainly in the system test area, when volume, stress and response are being tested.

The IT Infrastructure Library
Testing an IT Service for Operational Use

Performance measurement tools may be used to identify errors in the design and implementation of an IT service and its databases which lead to bottlenecks, excessive disk capacity and usage and many other operational problems. They may point to errors in the way in which databases have been set up for operational use. In extreme circumstances they may even uncover errors in programming styles, such as the use of very inefficient language facilities.

Bespoke tools may be required for specific projects. For example, if the introduction of a new system requires data to be converted from old databases, then tools will be required to perform the conversion process and check that it has been successful. Whilst file comparators may help with this type of work, it is unlikely that they will be able to handle comparisons between widely varying database structures, such as comparing an indexed sequential file with a relational database. Furthermore, data conversions may produce both technical and logical differences between the old and new databases which can only be resolved by a specially written utility.

8. Bibliography

Most books and papers on testing are concerned with testing in the development environment. Very little has been written on the subject of testing IT services for operational use. This bibliography has been selected on the basis that each book or paper has relevance to testing in general or to operational testing in particular.

Androile, S. J., Software Validation, Verification, Testing and Documentation, Petrocelli Books, 1986.

Beizer, B., Software Testing Techniques, 2nd edition, Van Nostrand Reinhold, 1990 - ISBN 0 442 206720.

CCTA: Improving the Maintainability of Software, HMSO, 1993 - ISBN 0 11 330585 0.

Fenton, N. E., Software Metrics: a rigorous approach, Chapman & Hall, 1991 - ISBN 0 412 40440 0.

Graham, D. R., Computer Aided Software Testing: CAST Report, Unicom Seminars Ltd, 1991.

Graham, D. R., Software Testing Tools: A new classification scheme, Journal of Software Testing, Verification and Reliability, Vol 1, Issue 2.

Hetzel, W. C., The Complete Guide to Software Testing, QED, 2nd edition, 1988.

Kaner, C., Testing Computer Software, TAB Professional and Reference Books, 1988.

McCabe, T. J. (Ed.), Structured Testing, IEEE, 1983.

Myers, G. J., The Art of Software Testing, John Wiley & Sons Inc., 1979 - ISBN 0 471 04328 1.

The following will be of relevance to organizations incorporating their operational testing functions within a Quality Management System.

CCTA, Quality Management Library, HMSO, 1992 - ISBN 0 11 330569 9.

Further information on Usability Testing (described in Annex G), can be found in the following papers.

Velotta, C. (managing editor), Practical Approaches to Usability Testing for Technical Documentation, Society for Technical Communications, 901 N. Stuart Street, Arlington, VA22203, USA. 1993.

Ramsey, J., A Selected Bibliography: A Beginner's Guide to Usability Testing, *and*
Rosenbaum, S., Usability Evaluations Versus Usability Testing: When & Why?
Usability Testing, IEEE Transactions on Professional Communication, 32(4), 1989.

Spencer, R., Computer Usability: Testing & Evaluation, Prentice Hall, 1985.

Annex A. Glossary of terms

Acronyms and abbreviations used in this module

ANSI	American National Standards Institution
BCS	British Computer Society
BSI	British Standards Institution
CASE	Computer Aided Software Engineering
CAST	Computer Aided Software Testing
CM	Configuration Management
FM	Facilities Management
IEEE	Institution of Electrical and Electronic Engineers
IS	Information System
IT	Information Technology
JCL	Job Control Language
MTBF	Mean Time Between Failures
PC	Personal Computer
PER	Project Evaluation Review
PIR	Post Implementation Review
PRINCE	PRojects In Controlled Environments
SDLC	Software Development LifeCycle
SLA	Service Level Agreement
SSADM	Structured Systems Analysis and Design Method
VDU	Visual Display Unit

Definitions used in this module

Beta site testing	The use of a site or installation independent of the software development site for running operational tests.
Black box testing	Testing which uses no knowledge of the internal structure or logic of a system.

The IT Infrastructure Library
Testing an IT Service for Operational Use

Bug	An error in programming code, producing an undesirable variation from design performance in a program during execution.
Error	Any non-conformance between software and either its specification, design or implementation, or its behaviour as stated or implied by users and operation staff.
Parameter file	A file, external to the software program, containing information required by the IT service to run correctly.
Regression testing	Testing undertaken to prove that changes introduced to the system do not affect the way in which the remainder of the system performs.
Regression pack	A series of test cases which tests specific functions of the system.
Software Maintenance *(IEEE definition)*	Any modification of a software product after delivery to correct faults, to improve performance or other attributes or to adapt the product to a changed environment.
Software supplier	The organization or company responsible for supplying software for operational testing. This may include an in-house software development or maintenance group, a software house or an agent for software distribution.
Test cycle	A test cycle is the single execution of a set of test runs contained in one stage of operational testing.
Test requirements	Test requirements are the highest level of description of the testing required for an IT service. They are based upon an analysis of the software requirements. For example, if a software requirement is to process a particular type of business transaction, then the test requirement will define the overall approach to testing that transaction.
Validation *(ISO9000-3 definition)*	The process of evaluating software to ensure compliance with specified requirements.
Verification *(ISO9000-3 definition)*	The process of evaluating the products of a given phase to ensure correctness and consistency with respect to the products and standards provided as input to that phase.
White box testing	Testing which is based upon knowledge of the internal structure and logic of a system.

Annex B. Software lifecycles and operational testing

B.1 Introduction

A theme which runs throughout this module is that test activities start at the earliest development stages. That is, operational testing is not a separate stage which follows development, but is an integral part of it. The consequence is that testers must understand the software lifecycle model being used in a project, and should be assured that they have the correct opportunities to participate in the relevant stages.

It is beyond the scope of the module to discuss the various lifecycle models in detail but more information can be found in the **Software Lifecycle Support** module.

To plan and implement operational testing it is necessary to understand how testing activities are mapped onto the software development lifecycle (SDLC). Following is an example based upon the V-model of testing activities.

B.2 The V-model of testing activities

Figure B1, overleaf, shows a simplified version of the V-model of test activities. The major features of this model are that:

* tests are specified, designed and written in parallel with the software development lifecycle

* the relationship between the planning and execution of different types of testing are clearly identified

* during the testing phase, tests are run in the order of unit, integration, system, installation and acceptance.

Specifying and designing tests early in the SDLC is a very powerful method of finding errors in software requirements. It can be done without increasing the total development time, but will help find errors much earlier in the SDLC. Furthermore test specifications and designs can be subjected to the same quality control activities as the corresponding software documents, eg structured walkthrough or Fagan's Inspection.

In figure B1, a simplified SDLC is shown, based upon the Waterfall lifecycle model. In any development project, it is essential that this concept of specifying and designing tests early in the SDLC is applied to the actual lifecycle model being used.

The IT Infrastructure Library
Testing an IT Service for Operational Use

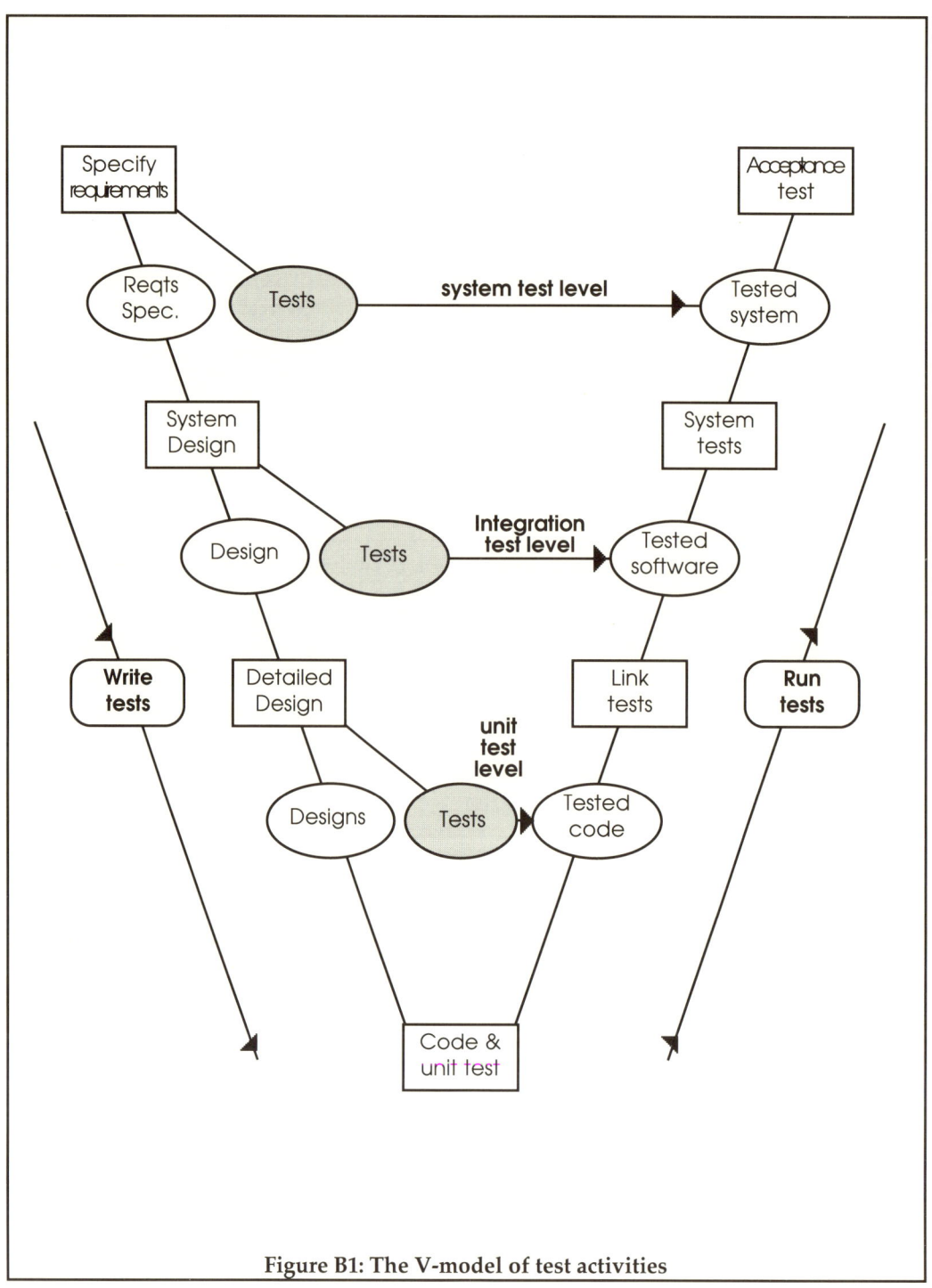

Figure B1: The V-model of test activities

Annex B
Software lifecycles and operational testing

The Software Lifecycle Support module describes the most common models, which are:

* Waterfall
* Spiral
* Evolutionary
* Rapid prototyping.

Each model describes the development stages in different ways, and some include stages not shown in the figure, such as modelling and benchmarking. Therefore an organization needs to develop its own version(s) of the V-model tailored to the SDLC(s) being used.

B.3 Participation of operational testing in the SDLC

During requirements capture, test analysts will need to determine the overall test requirements for the proposed software development project. Using the procedures in section 3 the test manager will draft an initial test plan describing general goals, broad estimates of resources and costs, and the proposed test strategy requirements.

During the specification stage, test analysts should be involved in reviews to ensure that test requirements are being addressed within the specifications. As specifications become more detailed, testers can provide further input to the review processes based upon their own knowledge of errors which have been found in other software.

Since there is a strong correlation between the software's design and its test suite, test suite design should commence while software design is still in progress. Test designers should participate in design reviews, firstly to ensure that the designs meet any test requirements, and secondly to contribute their experience of design errors. As design work becomes more detailed so test case design may similarly proceed. The involvement of test personnel during the design phase can make a significant contribution to the testability of the final design.

For more information about testability, please refer to Annex C, which discusses Quality, Testability and Dependability.

The IT Infrastructure Library
Testing an IT Service for Operational Use

It is unlikely that all test design work will be completed at this stage. Although the work done will probably represent the basis of the final test suite, there are at least three factors which imply additional design work later in the lifecycle:

* user manuals, which may be the basis for some of the user and system tests, may not be finalized until development testing (unit and link tests) of the software is complete

* it may not be possible to design some of the installation tests until the final configuration details are known

* during the course of operational testing, staff must have the freedom to design new test cycles if circumstances dictate.

The detailed involvement of the operational testing function with software development should be documented as part of the project quality plan. Software development management are responsible for the quality plan. The plan should be derived initially from an organization's quality management system, which documents the parts of the plan to be drafted by the test manager.

Annex C. Quality, testability and dependability

C.1 Introduction

This annex discusses the positioning of testing an IT service for operational use within a quality culture and how it fits within a Quality Management System (QMS). A QMS will contain provision for the planning of adequate testing.

C.2 Quality

C.2.1 Quality definitions

ISO8402 defines quality as "the totality of features and characteristics of a product or service that bear upon its ability to satisfy stated or implied needs".

This definition can be recognized, in everyday terms, as requiring "fitness for purpose", thus reinforcing the essential concept that in order to judge the quality of a product or service, it is necessary to know the purpose for which that product or service is required. There is, however, the recognition that this purpose may not be explicitly stated, and that a complete and unambiguous statement of requirements is not always achievable.

In operational testing, it is necessary to test many attributes of an IT service other than its functions. Some of these attributes may be difficult to define in a specification; eg those relating to the human factors involved with running an IT service. This can to some extent be addressed by techniques such as usability testing where in effect the IT service is tested against a representative sample of users, whose attitudes, abilities and intuitive assumptions constitute the requirement to be satisfied (see Annex G).

C.2.2 Quality aims

The aim of the QMS should be recognized by all staff involved with the testing of an IT service for operational use. This aim will relate to the need to produce, first time, a service that meets the defined needs, including the requirements of testability and dependability.

Given that testing can never be totally comprehensive, if costs are to be realistic, then errors will occur. One role of a QMS is to assist in establishing an acceptable level of errors in each element of an IT service, and ensure that this level is not exceeded.

The IT Infrastructure Library
Testing an IT Service for Operational Use

Testing is concerned to demonstrate acceptability in terms of the declared quality characteristics, including:

* usability
* functionality
* maintainability
* portability
* availability
* durability
* responsiveness
* accessibility
* dependability.

C.2.3 Basic quality rules

Finally, there are several rules which apply to any quality control activity, and especially to operational testing. These are:

* no testing without measurable objectives
* no testing without recording
* no recording without analysis
* no analysis without action.

These rules encapsulate the feedback principle which is essential to any quality activity. It is recommended that an operational testing function should apply these rules rigorously.

The purpose of feedback is to enable:

* errors to be removed, thereby improving the quality of the IT service
* improvements to be made to the software development processes so that more errors can be prevented earlier in the SDLC
* the testing procedures themselves to be improved.

Annex C
Quality, testability and dependability

C.3 Testability

Definition

The testability of an IT service is the ease with which errors can be located and the confidence which can be placed in the assertion that the IT service meets its specification and the other performance criteria.

Testability is an inherent characteristic of software, and the following key factors will contribute to it.

Effects of software design

Software has to be designed so that it is testable. A great deal has been written about software design criteria, but one of the most important concepts is that software should be built from small, well defined building blocks. This approach minimizes the complexity of individual parts of a software system, thereby avoiding large monolithic systems of high complexity.

Complexity can be considered as an inverse measure of testability, albeit not the only measure. For example, a large and complex program with many thousands of test paths may be untestable because it is not practicable to perform such a large number of test cases. By comparison, a large program built from small, well defined, modules is a much better proposition as it is easier to test a larger number of simple modules than a single very complex one.

For example if a program has 1000 test paths, then a single test of the program will require a minimum of 1000 test cases and this will require a very large test effort, and significant time to analyze the results. If changes are made to the code, all of the test may have to be repeated because the code is a monolithic block, and it may be virtually impossible to determine which test paths were affected by the changes. If the program consisted of 50 code procedures each with 20 test paths, then each code procedure can be tested individually, and then the links between the code procedures tested. The test workload now consists of a number of manageable test runs. If changes are made to a code procedure, then only the paths in that code procedure need to be retested. The links to other code procedures can be tested separately.

If program testing is made unnecessarily difficult through poor structure, then it is likely that more errors will find their way through to the operational testing stages. When errors have been found, corrections will be more error prone, retesting will be more difficult and this may result in even more errors in software passed to operational testing. Consequently, operational testers have a significant interest in the ability of development staff to perform their test activities successfully.

Effects of software lifecycles

An appropriate SDLC should be used which allows for testing staff to be involved from the earliest stages of development. Annex B discusses the use of the V-model as a means of planning test activities in conjunction with the SDLC. At every stage in the SDLC, testing staff should be asking the question, "How will I test this?".

If the wrong SDLC is chosen then attempts may be made to complete the specification stage prematurely. The result will be unstable specifications which undergo an unacceptable number of changes due to problems encountered in the design and coding stages. Consequently, tests will need constant revision.

Documentation

Specifications, user manuals and other documentation must represent the final state of the IT service, notwithstanding the many changes made during development. Whilst specifications alone are insufficient to develop all of the test cases for operational testing, they do provide the starting point.

C.3.1 Maintainability

The concepts and requirements that make software inherently testable are fundamentally identical to those which produce maintainable software. The techniques and considerations relating to this are addressed in considerable detail in the CCTA publication **Improving the Maintainability of Software**. Software that is developed in accordance with that guidance will be high in testability as well as maintainability.

C.4 Dependability

Section 3 describes the need for a risk analysis in order to determine how an organization may be affected by failures within an IT service, and how to estimate the risks posed to the business. Rather than concentrate on risk, and the negative aspects this reveals, it can be more constructive to consider the dependability of the product. Operational testing should be designed to assess the dependability of an IT service.

Annex C
Quality, testability and dependability

Dependability is defined in ISO8402 as "the collective term used to describe the availability performance and its influencing factors: reliability performance, maintainability performance and maintenance support performance". The dependability of software will be a major influence upon the benefit (or liability) that it is to the business user and therefore testing aimed at establishing the likely dependability of a product or service is, in itself, an asset to an organization.

C.4.1 When to stop testing

Establishing dependability requires knowledge of when sufficient testing has been performed so that the IT service can confidently be released for operational running. There are a number of methods for determining when to stop testing, but some are not acceptable as they do not take the quality of the testing performed into account.

There are particular concerns relating to the testing of urgent and emergency changes to an IT service. The following sections discuss methods for determining when to stop testing, and how to handle the risks associated with change.

C.4.1.1 Methods to be avoided

Time limited testing

One method is simply to set a time limit for test runs. This is not considered acceptable for three main reasons:

* time alone is not a measure of test coverage or test quality; it is acknowledged that plans must contain estimates of the time required for test runs; however, when this time has been expended it does not mean that testing can stop

* test running takes place late in the SDLC, and any overruns in earlier stages may threaten the time allowed for this test work

* time must be allowed for finding and fixing errors, and this is difficult to estimate accurately; any fixed times allocated for testing are unlikely to contain sufficient provision for remedial action and retesting.

Testing by quantity not quality

Another method is to end test running when all test cycles can be completed with no errors found, but without due consideration of how many errors have been found overall. The problem with this idea is that it places more emphasis on the number of tests runs which do not find errors, and does not relate to the quality of the testing, noting that good testing should find as many errors as possible. This criterion may lead testers, unconsciously, to design tests which are not good at finding errors, which is exactly the opposite of what is required.

C.4.1.2 Methods to consider

Estimating likely error levels

One acceptable method is based upon the numbers of errors found during testing. For example, from experiences of testing IT services in other, similar projects, it may be possible to estimate the likely numbers of errors which may be in the software when it is passed to operational testing. Therefore measures can be used to compare the number of errors found with those anticipated, and some level determined at which acceptable test coverage has been achieved. The value of this approach is that it is consistent with the main emphasis of operational testing which is that of finding errors.

Reliability modelling

A more refined method is to use reliability modelling to determine the probability of failure. A reliability model is based on data obtained by recording how long an IT service runs before each error is found. As more errors are found and removed, so the mean time between failure (MTBF) will increase. The modelling method produces a graph which shows how the reliability changes over a period of running. This graph can be used to determine when sufficient test runs have been performed by showing that the MTBF of the IT service has reached the required value for operational running.

Reliability models can be used in two ways:

* during test running, a graph can be used to show how reliability is changing, to predict how long it will be before the IT service reaches the required MTBF, and determine when that point has been reached

* during operational service, a graph can be used to measure the actual reliability of the IT service, which may well be different from the reliability measured during testing.

Annex C
Quality, testability and dependability

A comparison of these two MTBF figures will provide a measure of the effectiveness of operational testing.

Some models require specialist mathematical skills which may not be available within an IT Directorate. Consequently it is recommended that the method is used in a simpler form.

For example, a graph plotting the number of errors found against testing time, or numbers of test cases executed, will show whether the IT service is becoming more or less reliable. In an ideal situation, the number of errors found should decrease over time, indicating that the risk of future failure is diminishing. When the risk of failure is considered acceptably low, testing can be considered complete.

Even though models like this may provide a more manageable way of assessing risk and the effectiveness of the testing process, it will be necessary to exercise caution when interpreting their results. Errors may have a widely varying impact on the IT service's operation, and therefore any modelling should take into account the nature and severity of different types of error. It may be worth ignoring trivial and cosmetic errors, and only considering more severe errors in the modelling process. Annex E gives an example of error severity classes (E.4) and from the table, which has 5 classes, only errors of severity 1 to 3 may be important for reliability modelling.

Reliability modelling offers other benefits as well. Indirectly it measures the ability of test runs to find errors during the testing phase of a project. If many test runs are performed, and few errors are found, then this may indicate to management that either the IT service is generally error-free, or that testing is inadequate. Management can then look for evidence which corroborates one or other view from other quality control activities.

Other methods

Other acceptable methods may be based upon valid criteria such as:

* measuring test coverage, eg the number and types of tests applied to each function being tested

* using a range of test techniques which have been shown to be effective

* error seeding, eg introduce specific types of errors into the software, and see if they are detected.

C.4.2 The risk of change

When an IT service is in operation, further risks arise in determining the impact of changes and the degree of regression testing required, and in the handling of emergency fixes.

Determining the impact of a change on the IT service, and therefore identifying the breadth and depth of testing required, depends upon the maintainability and testability of the software and documentation involved. This is a further reason why testers should be involved in the early development stages, as there is always a need for some degree of risk assessment. If reliability modelling is used throughout the operational life of an IT service, then the effects of past changes on reliability can be measured, and judgments made as to the quality of the tests performed. When a new change has to be made, past history may indicate where extra test effort is needed.

The decision whether to implement an emergency fix poses a difficult operational problem, as there are risks in either case. There may be significant risks to business operations if an error is not fixed quickly allowing the operational service to be resumed with minimum delay. There may also be the risks associated with making corrections when the amount of testing that can be performed is limited by time. The dilemma is how to balance these risks realistically and so to take decisions which minimize the overall risk.

There is no easy answer to this problem, as every emergency fix has to be judged in its own immediate context. There are, however, several factors which can help to alleviate this situation.

Good testability — If software has good testability, then this will help testers to identify the minimum depth and breadth of testing required, and therefore keep a limited test effort focused on the fix.

Regression packs — If comprehensive and flexible regression test packs have been developed, then testers may be able to select a minimum set of regression tests for use within a fixed time which will help increase confidence. However, it is acknowledged that test selection under pressure is a difficult task. An alternative tactic is to develop what some may know as a 'flash test'. This is a test suite which can be run in a short time to test the major processing functions of the IT service. After an emergency fix has been made, the flash test may give some degree of confidence that no major

Annex C
Quality, testability and dependability

errors have been introduced elsewhere in the IT service. The use of fully automated regression testing packs may mean it becomes possible to run a complete regression test quickly and easily.

Continue testing

Testing should not stop just because an emergency fix has been released, instead comprehensive test runs should be started without delay with the aim of finding any errors before they occur in operation. In some circumstances, the fix may only be temporary, in which case the software maintainers may need to design and implement a permanent fix as a priority. Consequently, additional test runs will need to be planned and executed in parallel.

Annex D. Checklists of basic handover requirements

D.1 Introduction

The following are checklists of handover requirements from software development to operational testing, and from operational testing to software control and distribution following the completion of acceptance test runs. In organizations with mature quality management systems, the handover criteria should already be documented. For those not in this position, the lists are meant as an aid to developing an in-house set.

All handovers of software from one stage to another should be controlled using the configuration management system. This is necessary so as to:

* ensure that all the configuration items have been identified and handed over
* provide an audit trail for the items
* prevent unauthorized changes being made to any items whilst test running is being performed.

D.2 Handover to operational testing

Handover from software development to operational testing:

* confirmation of configuration - a definitive list of all configuration items handed over
* software requirements and specification documents
* software design documents
* source code files and accompanying documentation
* object code and executable files
* job control libraries
* confirmation of successful completion of development tests
* specification of allowable configurations
* software build and installation instructions, and associated installation routines

- user manuals
- manuals for use by computer operations staff
- technical support manuals
- regression test sets
- records of all errors found during development test runs and their associated change history.

D.3 Handover to software control and distribution

Handover to software control and distribution following the completion of operational test runs:

- the final versions of all the items listed above, plus
- confirmation of successful completion of system tests
- confirmation of successful completion of installation tests
- confirmation of successful completion of acceptance tests
- all test plans, specifications, designs and test suites used during operational testing
- records of all errors found during operational test runs and their associated change history.

D.4 General handover issues

During operational testing runs, errors will be found and changes will be made to individual configuration items, eg specifications or source code files. Changes made by the software development staff should be subject to both change and configuration management. This will ensure the integrity of the final configuration which is accepted by the users, and handed over to software control and distribution.

There will be a requirement for the internal handover of a software system from one stage of operational testing to another. For example, acceptance test runs should not commence until system and installation test runs have been completed and signed off.

Annex D
Checklists of basic handover requirements

There are several ways in which this internal control may be exercised, and they depend upon the way in which configuration management is organized. For example:

* there may be a single operational testing environment, in which case internal control procedures within the operational testing function are required for authorizing the movement of software from one stage of operational testing to another

* there may be separate testing environments for each of the three stages of systems, installation and acceptance test running, in which case the handover of a system from one stage to another can be controlled using the configuration management system.

Annex E. The principles of good testing

The bibliography lists several books that discuss various aspects of testing. Much of what is written is biased towards testing in a software development environment rather than for operational use. However many of the basic principles are common. Among these books 'The Complete Guide to Software Testing' by Hetzel, 'Managing the Software Process' by Humphrey and 'Testing Computer Software' by Kaner give good practical guidance. The principles listed here are widely accepted and should form a basis for the activities of any test group.

Whilst there is good guidance available on the principles of test design, one area that is often overlooked is that of managing the test environment. This management task can vary widely in complexity depending on the size of the IT service, both in terms of software and hardware. Therefore this section gives additional guidance on this topic.

In summary, this section discusses:

* preparing test plans
* designing test suites
* preparing and executing test runs
* analyzing test results
* managing the test environment.

E.1 Preparing test plans

As previously emphasized, test planning must start early. Operational testing personnel should be involved when the requirements specification of a new IT service or upgrade is being prepared. The first draft of the test plan should be drawn up at the same time. As the software specifications and detailed designs are produced so the test plan should be revised in step with them.

Test plans should detail the testing strategy, the test designs, responsibilities, deliverables, procedures and controls. The contents should be reviewed by the project designers and users.

Detailed plans should be structured. Each test should have its input data defined and will produce output. If the input data is independent of any other tests in the plan then all tests can be run independently to maximize the number of errors found on each pass through the plan. This in turn allows the fixing of as many errors as possible by development teams before resubmission for operational testing. The first tests in the plan should test the individual processes of each function with later tests checking that data can be taken through a number of processes in one test.

Test cases should be prioritized to ensure that the most important test objectives are met first. That way rejection will occur earlier rather than later. Early rejection tends to save time and effort on unproductive testing. For example, testing should start first on core software, such as database management software.

It should be remembered that test plans are based upon specific versions of a software system. Therefore they must be included as 'configuration items' in a configuration management and change control system to ensure that they remain in step with software versions.

E.2 Designing test suites

Designing good test suites is at the heart of successful testing. The design criteria are considered under two headings:

* test suite design

* test case design.

It is emphasized that test suite design starts in the early stages of development, and is performed in parallel with software design and implementation.

E.2.1 Test suite design

It is recommended that any test suite should be decomposed into a number of test cycles. The main design characteristics of each test cycle are:

* a well defined scope; i.e. the cycle tests a specific part of the software, or a particular attribute of an IT service such as volume or performance

* independence from other test cycles, so that any desired combination of test cycles can be performed to meet a specific test requirement

Annex E
The principles of good testing

* maintainability, that is when an IT service is changed, the changes required to test cycles are localized

* simplicity, which is allied to scope, and means that test cycles are kept reasonably short.

There is a clear parallel between systems design and test suite design. Test suites may be designed by using several decomposition techniques. For example, from software specifications it should be possible to develop transaction flow charts. Test cycles can then be developed to test individual transactions. This is a functional approach to testing.

As stated earlier, a considerable part of operational testing is concerned with validating aspects of an IT service which may not be described in detail in specifications.

Validation includes tests of the IT service from the user's viewpoint; therefore to design test cycles for this work requires their involvement. User manuals and other documentation should be used to develop cycles which mirror the way in which the user expects to use the IT service.

There are specialist areas, such as performance and operability, where other IT service management functions may need to contribute to test suite design. For example, performance tests cannot be carried out simply by running an IT service in isolation, as the measured performance will depend partly on the characteristics of the IT service under test, and partly upon the general machine loading at the time the tests are performed. Performance analysts will be required to develop test cycles which account for these factors. They will also be needed to interpret the results, and separate global performance problems from those which apply to the IT service under test.

It is not generally possible to design a test suite for operational testing in a single pass. Suites may have to be developed incrementally as testers gain experience and understanding of the IT service. For example, early test cycles may indicate a particular weakness in the design of a software system. This information can then help the testers to design additional test cycles to investigate this weakness and thereby identify as many errors as possible which are symptomatic of it.

E.2.2 Test case design

Design considerations

The fundamental problem of software testability (discussed in Annex C3) is that, except in the most trivial cases, it is not possible to fully test software. Consequently, several techniques have been developed for obtaining maximum test coverage from a limited number of test cases. They are discussed briefly here, but the bibliography contains several texts, such as Myers' 'The Art of Software Testing', where more detail can be found. However, first of all it is necessary to consider the characteristics of a good test case, which are:

* it has a high probability of detecting a previously undetected defect, not one that shows that the program works correctly
* it embodies a description of the expected output
* it gives reproducible results
* it must check for invalid as well as valid input conditions.

There are further characteristics, which are discussed in the following paragraphs about individual design methods.

Equivalence partitioning

The first of the well documented design methods is known as equivalence partitioning. In this approach, possible test cases are identified using two criteria:

* as many different input conditions as possible are tested
* each test case represents a class of conditions.

For example, an input may have a valid range of 1 to 999. Test cases could be designed for:

* input of 1 and 999, which test the bounds of the input
* input of 2, 10, 100, 355, 566, 777 and 998 which test valid inputs not at the bounds, but are representative of all valid values from 2 to 998 (seven test cases are used to represent the possible 997 values)
* input of 0 and 1000, which tests the invalid input conditions, but where the input is not negative
* input of -1 and -999, which tests for invalid negative input.

Annex E
The principles of good testing

If the input variable is an integer with a possible range of -32767 to +32768, then equivalence partitioning will identify a small number of test cases which test the main valid and invalid input classes without the need to try every possible input value.

Boundary condition analysis

A complementary method to the previous one is boundary condition analysis. As the name suggests, test cases are designed around the bounds of input data. For example, if an input has a valid range of £1.00 to £999.00 then test cases can be written for input values such as £0.99, £1.00, £1.01, £998.99, £999.00 and £999.01. This method is frequently advocated as an efficient error-finding approach.

Error guessing

Another technique, which is less formal, is that of error guessing. This is an intuitive technique which is acquired rather than taught. It relies on a tester's ability to think laterally and identify unusual processing situations. As such, it is similar in some aspects to equivalence partitioning.

A simple example is that of the test cases to apply to a sort routine. Apart from normal test cases, exceptional cases may include when:

* the sort file is empty
* there is only one record
* all entries are the same
* the file is already in sorted order.

Error guessing may be particularly useful when designing test cases which reflect the way a user may operate the IT service.

Cause-effect graphing

A fourth technique is that of cause-effect graphing. This technique requires the tester to develop logic diagrams which show how the effects of different input conditions combine. The strength of the method over the others described so far is its emphasis on trying to find combinations of input conditions which represent classes of input. However, a similar result can be achieved by using decision tables as the basis for generating test cases. This is a particularly useful technique for the validation of complex data, eg cheque clearance.

The IT Infrastructure Library
Testing an IT Service for Operational Use

For example, a program may require two inputs, one of which can have discrete values, eg 1, 2 and 3, and the other a range, eg 100 to 200. A cause-effect graph can be developed to show how the IT service should react to various combinations of these inputs. The test cases should be designed to find errors in the way that the software handles different combinations of inputs. If both inputs are invalid, does the software report this, or only report the first invalid one it encounters? Another example is that of mutually dependent fields, where input values may be correct individually, but not when considered in combination.

Taken to extremes, with an on-line screen which requires many values, does the screen accept them all, and then produce an error only for the first invalid one?, or does it validate each one as input? This is an important example of error handling, as poor error handling can make an IT service difficult to use. Whilst error handling should be described in a specification, it is an area which is difficult to define precisely. This is because it is relatively simple to state the positive functions of an IT service, but significantly more difficult to identify what may go wrong during processing, and determine how the software should behave in all error situations.

In deciding the acceptability of an IT service, operational testers will need to draw upon their knowledge of the context in which the IT service is likely to be used and the attitude of the users. Those users should, therefore, be involved throughout the testing process. Usability testing (see Annex G) can help in gathering the knowledge of users in a formal and structured way.

General design principles

Apart from these techniques, there are other, more general, principles which are worth noting. They include:

* ensure good coverage when designing test cases; this can be assisted by

    - using the specifications and user documentation as a basis for designing test cases (note that if the user documentation is used as a basis for test cases then the tests will detect errors in both software and documentation)

    - looking for aspects that are not covered

    - making use of checklists (available from several books)

Annex E
The principles of good testing

* check that functions within the IT service operate correctly when repeated as well as the first time around

* check that functions operate correctly irrespective of the order in which they are performed

* test all functions

* test all classes of inputs and outputs

* look for the limits and test what happens at and beyond the limits.

It is worth noting that the techniques described above are known as 'black box' techniques. They assume no knowledge of the internal structure or logic of the software. By comparison, developers and maintainers may perform 'white box' testing as part of verification testing, where test cases are designed to test the paths, branches and other structural elements of the internal design of the software. These two different approaches characterize a major difference between verification and validation.

E.3 Preparing and executing test runs

There are a number of general considerations which apply to the preparation and execution of test runs. Whilst some of them may seem obvious, they should not be overlooked:

* ensure the availability of the test plan

* prepare test data in advance

* ensure availability and check configuration of software under test

* ensure availability of hardware and tools

* set up and check the test environment

* load the initial data files

* input the test data

* observe carefully what happens during the test run

* log the test run noting any peculiarities or problems that arise

* record the results and check against the expected results recorded in the test plan

* clean up the test environment.

The penultimate point above is worthy of greater emphasis because it embodies the quality principle of 'not testing without recording'. The test records are the key output, and the essential input to the next step. Any variation should be noted. Where variations do occur then the test should be repeated to ensure that the variation is reproducible. Often, performing a test can lead to observations on details that are not directly the subject of the test. Such observations should also be noted and explored further. Experimentation may well lead to the uncovering of unexpected errors and is to be encouraged. When such experimentation does take place the procedures should ensure that the results are used to update the test plan

E.4 Analyzing test results

Whilst a great deal of care and effort may have been invested in designing and executing a test suite, it is the review of the test results which will start to give a return on this investment. The following are some suggested principles for analyzing results.

At the end of each pass through the test plan, the errors found should be sorted and prioritized. Sort into software or documentation errors requiring the attention of the software development team, and suggested modifications. Test runs may also identify errors in the tests themselves. Reports of errors should be passed to the appropriate software development or maintenance teams for correction. Modifications should be handled through the change control procedures. Testing of this part of the software should then stop until the next release is supplied.

Use of a simple, formal, rating system can help prioritize errors. A typical five point system is shown at figure E.1 as an example.

When using such a system remember that priorities can differ depending on the perspective of the person affected by the error, eg a user may be able to live with a particular report not being in the required format but it may have a higher priority in the eyes of the business manager. Furthermore a minor error may impede operational testing and therefore require higher priority. Consequently the form used to record errors might include the viewpoint of those affected.

Additional value can be obtained from test results by analyzing the nature of the error. This is particularly important from a quality management viewpoint, as the

Annex E
The principles of good testing

severity code	example
1	a function fails with no work-round, compromising or degrading an essential feature of the system
2	a function fails and no acceptable work-round is available
3	a function fails and an acceptable work-round is available
4	a function works in a way which reduces the user's productivity
5	aesthetic and other minor problems

Figure E.1: A typical severity code system

nature of an error should indicate where it was introduced, and allow management to review the development stage or activity which generated it. For example an error may be caused by an error in the original specification, or in the various design stages, or during coding. Also errors should be examined to see if they should have been detected by earlier test stages, and if so, why testing failed to reveal them at that stage.

At the end of each pass through the test plan an End Stage Assessment meeting should be held at which the project board receives a report from the test manager and makes a decision on whether or not the IT service can be formally accepted and passed to the next stage. In some circumstances a conditional acceptance may be granted. This should only be done if the remaining problems are minor, and the risk is considered low.

The summary effect of these principles is to provide management with comprehensive information on the number and types of errors in an IT service. Without this, management cannot take effective corrective action, or determine when risks are low enough for testing to finish.

E.5 Managing the test environment

The main considerations of managing a test environment are:

* using configuration management services
* environment design

The IT Infrastructure Library
Testing an IT Service for Operational Use

* environment operation
* environment maintenance.

Due to the widely varying size and complexity of information systems, it is not possible to give definitive solutions for the management task. Instead, the principles of test management are discussed, so that they can be applied to individual situations.

E.5.1 Using configuration management services

The design, operation and maintenance of a test environment depends very much on the configuration management (CM) facilities available.

It is assumed that some form of CM is in use throughout the software development lifecycle, as it is not considered feasible to manage a development project without one. It is also assumed that CM is implemented using software tools, as it is also considered impracticable to operate CM on a purely manual basis.

The use of CM is essential for:

* keeping operational test plans, documentation and test suites in step with software versions
* providing management reports on the status of configuration items.

Whilst the use of CM is discussed generally in the following sections, reference should be made to the IT Infrastructure Library module on **Configuration Management** for full details of a CM function.

E.5.2 Test environment design

The main design principles are that:

* wherever possible, the test environment is independent from development and live environments but noting that there will be instances where test runs have to be performed in the live environments, eg to run tests on a network, where the network cannot be simulated
* access to the environment is strictly controlled, both in terms of its external interfaces with other configuration environments, and in terms of the modification and use of software libraries within the environment

Annex E
The principles of good testing

* within the environment, libraries are structured to meet the following requirements

    - there should be a set of master test libraries for each development project, each master set containing the definitive software configuration handed over to operational testing

    - that within the master set for an individual project, separate libraries are used to store different classes of files, eg source code files, executables, run jobs, test suites, databases and test documentation

* there are working sets of libraries for each project in which individual tests can be configured and run without affecting the master libraries, or other test runs being performed in the same project

* the configuration of test runs and their execution should be automated wherever possible, using a test scheduler, for three reasons

    - to be efficient

    - to provide reproducibility

    - to enable any tester to run or rerun a particular set of tests.

Test reproducibility is a vital factor in successful operational testing. If a test which finds an error cannot be rerun in exactly the same way as it was originally, then it becomes very difficult not only to provide accurate diagnostic data for debugging purposes, but also to demonstrate that the error has been removed once the software has been amended. In a large software system, a test run may access many hundreds of files, and the only way to remove doubt as to whether the correct versions of these files were used is by automating the test build and execution process.

E.5.3 Test environment operation

Test environment operation is described in two parts:

* capacity management of the environment
* automated test scheduling and execution.

The IT Infrastructure Library
Testing an IT Service for Operational Use

E.5.3.1 Capacity Management

In order to operate a test environment effectively, consideration should be given to the following capacity issues:

* master test libraries may require a large storage capacity, and there should be fast access to this storage so that individual tests can be configured efficiently in the working libraries

* the working libraries, in which tests are run, may also require significant disk storage to cope with

  - the generation of large output files
  - situations where software errors create files much larger than expected

* working libraries may need to be configured for access to systems functions, such as a transaction processing monitor or a database management system, and there may be differences in which these systems functions are configured for operational use, and the way in which they need to be configured for operational testing

* test runs may require significant amounts of processing power to build a working library, to execute the tests and to perform post-test tasks such as file comparison.

Capacity Management staff should be involved both in the planning and monitoring of the computer capacity required to support operational testing. For further guidance, reference should be made to the **Capacity Management** and **Software Lifecycle Support** modules.

E.5.3.2 Automated test scheduling

In Annex E.5.2, the design requirement for automated test scheduling and execution was discussed. In terms of operation of the test environment it is recommended that a test scheduler is developed which can allow a tester to specify the:

* master test libraries from which the working library is to be built

* versions of input and database files which should be used, as well as master results files for comparison with those generated during the test run

Annex E
The principles of good testing

* modifications to any parameter files used by the software, eg date files
* file comparison options, which will depend on the file comparison tool being used
* record and playback options if automated interactive testing is being performed
* degree of detail to be recorded in test journals, eg a summary showing simply program entry and exit during the run, or fuller details echoing file assignments and input/output operations
* way in which error situations are to be handled, eg abort the test run if an error occurs, or skip to the next section of the job.

The implementation of a test scheduler may be a significant task. Whilst implementation depends on the specific hardware and systems software configuration, there are important common aspects of operation.

For example, from the various parameters that may be input, a scheduler needs, initially, to construct a variety of job control programs for building the working library, executing the test run and analyzing the results, and it then needs to run these jobs. With large test environments which contain hundreds of files in many libraries, a key aspect is the handling of filenames. For the automated construction and running of test jobs, care is needed in the use of logical and physical filenames in the job control programs, so that the physical names of files can be connected logically to the programs being tested without any manual intervention.

Another example is keeping working libraries tidy. After a test run has been completed, and the working libraries archived if required, then the working libraries need to be cleared out, so that no files are left which could affect future test runs.

E.5.4 Test environment maintenance

A major aspect of test environment maintenance is how to amend and update test data files, master comparison files and test run parameter files. As operational test running continues, so new test data sets are created, and changes made to existing ones.

The IT Infrastructure Library
Testing an IT Service for Operational Use

One example is that of running the test of an interactive program for the first time, using a record/playback tool. After the first test run has been completed, errors may be found, and there may be subsequent retesting of amended software until no errors are found. At this point, the test data files used by the record/playback tool now become a reference set, which can be used in further test runs if required. The movement of this set into a master reference library should be performed under configuration management control.

Another aspect is that of dealing with the volume of data that test environments generate. Whilst the latest versions of libraries may be kept on fast disk storage for immediate use, it is necessary to consider how both current and previous versions are archived. To determine an archive policy, consideration should be given to:

* how far back, historically, test libraries should be maintained, remembering that there may be occasions when it is necessary to repeat an earlier test run if an error which was thought to have been corrected suddenly reappears

* the requirements of an organization's contingency plan; that is, what files should be archived in order for an organization to be able to continue operational testing if there is a major disaster which requires temporary working on a backup computer system.

Annex F. Formal signing off procedures

Once operational testing has been satisfactorily completed and the project board has signed off this phase it is important to ensure that the relevant managers and divisions within the organization are informed. The checklists below give further guidance on the communications necessary.

F.1 System tests

After system testing, some or all of the following may need to be informed:

Installation test team	Installation routines can be finalized and final testing commence. Although installation routines may be produced and tested in parallel with other parts of the IT service, a final test should be carried out with the software in its final form.
Software control and distribution	If the result of the test is a completed upgrade to be distributed and there is no need for further testing, the software is now available for distribution.
Contingency planning	Upgraded backup systems may need to be planned and tested.
Capacity management	Capacity availability and/or requirements may change on completion of testing.
Computer operations management and network management	The new or upgraded software may be ready for installation and acceptance testing, which may need to be performed on a live network.
Cost management	No immediate further spending on system testing will be required. Note that there may be further spending if a need for re-testing is identified as a result of finding errors in installation or acceptance tests. In this situation any further spending should be accounted for separately to enable the costs of re-test to be identified. Knowing where these costs are incurred is an invaluable aid for future planning.

F.2 Installation tests

After installation testing, some or all of the following may need to be informed:

Acceptance test team	Although acceptance test planning and preparation may proceed while system and installation tests are in progress, the acceptance tests themselves should take place when all system and installation tests have been completed and signed off.

The IT Infrastructure Library
Testing an IT Service for Operational Use

Software control and distribution	With installation tests complete new software and upgrades are available for distribution.
Contingency planning	Upgraded backup systems may need to be planned and tested.
Computer operations & network management	The new or upgraded software may be ready for transfer to live running, which may be on a network.
Capacity management	Capacity requirements may change on completion of testing.
Cost management	No immediate further spend on installation testing. Note that there may be further spending if re-testing is required as a result of finding errors in acceptance tests. Any further spend should be accounted for separately to enable the costs of re-test to be identified.

F.3 Acceptance tests

After acceptance testing, some or all of the following may need to be informed:

Contingency planning manager	Upgraded backup systems may need to be planned and tested.
Computer operations & network management	The software is now ready to transfer to live running.
Capacity management	Capacity requirements may change on completion of testing.
Cost management	Unless the acceptance is conditional, there should be no further spend on testing. Suppliers need to issue an invoice and customers should expect to receive one.
Help Desk	Help Desk staff need to be aware that software has been passed to Software Control and Distribution in preparation for live running.

Annex G. Usability testing

G.1 Description

Usability testing is concerned with establishing the efficiency and effectiveness with which an information system can be used by its customers. The ethos behind such considerations is that an information system should reflect the way in which people work. IT in the past has earned a reputation for expecting people to adapt to the imposed IT services. As with all forms of testing, usability test running is merely the last stage of a process that runs throughout the lifecycle of a product or maintenance change. The purpose of this Annex is to introduce the concept of usability testing, and explain the benefits available to an organization from adopting this approach in addition to more traditional methods of testing software and IT services.

G.2 Definitions and scope

Usability testing has been defined as the "structured process of collecting information on specific issues from the intended users of the IT service being tested". At its most sophisticated this can involve formal laboratory trials on a representative selection of the potential user community. Several organizations have constructed purpose built laboratories costing tens of thousands of pounds but such investment is not essential for the investigation of usability to provide dividends in terms of the production of quality IT services. Many serviceable 'usability labs' comprise a meeting room fitted out with a few PCs.

As with all testing, the design of tests can have a constructive input to the design considerations for new or maintained IT services, revealing errors in specification and design before considerable expenditure on analysis and programming has started. Software usability testing will evaluate an IT service's presentation rather than its functionality, which will be established by more conventional testing methods. Presentation broadly covers the areas that users will touch, including:

* screens, menus and error messages
* documentation
* intuitiveness.

Usability testing will collect information concerning both **usability** and **usefulness**.

Usability covers areas such as:

* is it easy to learn?
* is it easy to use repeatedly?
* does its mode of use fit with the (non IT) systems it supports?
* is the documentation relevant and understandable to a typical user?

Usefulness concerns the ability of new or modified IT services to:

* fulfil a genuine work requirement
* provide a benefit for the organization
* do something users actually **want** done
* integrate with other associated functions.

G.3 Applicability

Usability testing can work well in concert with a prototyping approach to software development or maintenance. The formal gathering of data from a representative cross-section of users can greatly build (or destroy unjustified) confidence in the approach adopted and can be instrumental in the production of user-centred IT services. This is particularly beneficial where the service is designed for use in an area with which the software developers or maintainers are unfamiliar, for example:

* skilled specialist staff such as hospital consultants
* relatively unskilled/unsophisticated users such as selection staff/fork lift drivers in warehousing applications
* creative and/or specialist areas of work where the mind-set of users is likely to be considerably different from IT professionals eg architects or journalists.

EC Directive 90/270/EEC, which will be the subject of regulations in the Health and Safety at Work Etc Act, contains requirements relating to staff working with VDUs. Usability testing can be helpful in ensuring at an early stage that new and/or revised IT services comply with the appropriate legislation.

Annex G
Usability testing

G.4 Methods used in usability testing

Usability testing involves the structured consultation of users to ascertain whether the IT service (and associated documentation) will meet their requirements in terms of supporting their work function. Such data gathering may include:

* developing and using questionnaires in face-to-face interviews, written communication and/or telephone contacts with users

* analyzing user logs relating to earlier versions of the IT service (or similar products) or prototypes

* arranging focus groups of users, discussing the product

* carrying out expert and/or peer review

* observing users (in the field or laboratory)

* making comparative measurements of throughput.

G.5 Interface with problem management

Usability testing carried out on a live IT service can provide valuable information relating to planned future versions and/or enhancements. Information gathered from this exercise also forms a valuable input to the help desk and problem management functions, providing information on how users actually use an IT service, where they are most likely to encounter problems, what kind of information will help them etc.

The Help Desk can determine 'usability targets' which can lead to more efficient change management and software maintenance. An example would be the identification that 75% of calls on a given service are from staff who use the IT service less than once a month; future enhancements of the software or documentation could then concentrate on making the IT service easier to use by providing more intuitive commands and messages.

G.6 Summary

Usability testing can provide a useful addition to the traditional testing methods, in particular it assures that a product/service or a change to a product/service is tested by those who will use it and in the final context of the Information System (IT, clerical and human) of which it forms only a part. Many organizations incorporate usability testing in their operational testing and it is particularly relevant to IT services with a large user base and/or frequent new releases.

Further information on usability testing can be found in the publications referenced in the Bibliography.

IT Infrastructure Library
Testing an IT Service for Operational Use

Comments Sheet

CCTA hopes that you find this book both useful and interesting. We will welcome your comments and suggestions for improving it.
Please use this form or a photocopy, and continue on a further sheet if needed.

From:
        Name

        Organization

        Address

        Telephone

COVERAGE
Does the material cover your needs?
If not, then what additional material would you like included.

CLARITY
Are there any points which are unclear?
If yes, please detail where and why.

ACCURACY
Please give details of any inaccuracies found.

If more space is required for these or other comments, please continue overleaf.

IT Infrastructure Library
Testing an IT Service for Operational Use

Comments Sheet

OTHER COMMENTS

Return to: IT Infrastructure Management Services
               CCTA,
               Gildengate House
               Upper Green Lane
               NORWICH, NR3 1DW

Further information

Further information on the contents of this module can be obtained from:

IT Infrastructure Management Services
CCTA
Gildengate House
Upper Green Lane
NORWICH
NR3 1DW.

Telephone: 0603 694808
(GTN: 3014 4808)